Contents

Introduction

All the Scandinavian and northern countries—Shetland Islands, Iceland, Sweden, Norway, Estonia, Faroe Islands, Finland, and Denmark—share an inheritance of Viking traditions. This includes the use of beautifully ornate decoration depicting human forms, ferocious twisting and twining dragons, beasts, and plant shapes on wooden, woven, stone, and metal artifacts; a wealth of traditional handicrafts, such as weaving and rya; and a unique history of traditional knitting techniques such as twined and stranded knitwear. These countries also share geographical similarities: long, dark, extremely cold winters punctuated by the unique beauty of the northern lights, as well as the dependency on the sea, forests, and pastoral farmland for survival.

Opposite page: A house on the Swedish coast. This page, top: A festive garland hangs on a door in Finland. Bottom: The Norwegian tundra.

There is also a history of a collective Scandinavian love and appreciation of the natural world and a belief that all aspects of daily life should be enhanced through the use of beautiful everyday objects made from natural materials. *Hygge* (pronounced HOO-gah) is a Scandinavian word for this specific aesthetic that, although not easily translatable, can mean warmth, humor, comfort, tenderness, contentment, and well-being. It can be applied not only to things, which should be shared in a loving and generous way, but also to people and environments.

With this shared history, textile heritage, and joy of hygge, Scandinavia offers an intriguing fusion of old and new ideas. Inspired by these traditions, I have designed *Northern Knits Gifts* as a celebration of the handknitted gift. Traditional northern folk knitwear—socks, stockings, mittens, shawls, fisherman's sweaters, caps, and jackets—has a long association of being offered or exchanged as a gift, a practice that,

In the last thirty years or so, there has been a resurgence of interest in preserving knitting traditions and techniques that were in danger of dying out and being forgotten. Luckily, we are now more aware and reacquainted with these ancient techniques, and once again knitting from the past is much more prominent in the knitting of today. I am not trying to replicate or resurrect exactly the original knits that I have seen in museums or books, (although, the basic construction of knitted mittens, socks, hats, and sweaters have changed little over the decades), but rather to learn from and be inspired by them—and to make contemporary projects suited to today's knitters and today's homes.

as we are all familiar with, continues today. By using traditional techniques, we can create beautiful everyday objects and garments that lift our spirits and make the act of giving a more enjoyable and pleasurable experience.

When knitting these projects you are effectively creating gifts that encapsulate traditions and heritage. Gifts connect us with our past and our ancestors, and gifts celebrate the here and now. Using this book will help to keep knitting rooted in the everyday ritual of living, making, creating, and gifting for yourself, family, and friends.

Opposite page: Stockholm, Sweden, in winter. This page, top: A beautiful yellow church in Estonia. Bottom: A break in the clouds in Moskenes Harbor, Lofoten Islands, Norway.

About Traditional Techniques

In this collection,

I have used the instantly recognizable stranded or Fair Isle techniques for classic, bright, patterned knitwear and the ancient and beautiful Swedish twined or two-ended knitting technique to create a unique wonderfully firm and double-thick fabric that is ideal for making mittens and socks.

I have also adapted the rya technique, creating a simplified version that is suitable for using on knitwear.

Rya

Originating in Finland, a rya (or *ryijy*) is essentially a loom-woven textile with a linen warp onto which small bunches of woolen threads are knotted by hand. This process creates a shaggy wool pile. Rya creates wonderful rugs and blankets that originally were used for bedding and sleigh rides. Ryas are ideal for the severely harsh winter climate of the northern lands—not only durable and practical, but also exceptionally luxurious.

Early ryas were made from naturally occurring shades of wool. Gradually, plant dyes, such as birch leaves, barks, and cones were used to introduce color. Ryas were an essential and much prized part of a bride's dowry; they could be used as a currency and even used to pay taxes!

In Denmark, the rya was used more extensively in the form of cushion covers for use in sleighs and carriages and had long and short wool pile forming all, or accentuating parts, of the pattern.

Now, rya has become an art form throughout Scandinavia.

Rya Flower Cushion (see page 106) uses a simplified version of traditional rya weaving techniques, making it suitable for adding a touch of texture to knitted projects.

Simple rugs are transformed into superb art pieces that are no longer used, but rather hung on the wall.

A simplified version of this technique has been used in the Rya Flower Cushion (see page 106).

Two-Color Stranded & Fair Isle

Stranded and Fair Isle knitting are among the most recognizable of Nordic motifs: a pattern of two or more colors often rendered in intricate designs inspired by the natural world and ancient magical symbols. The knitting is worked seamlessly in the round, with the yarns not in use being carried across the wrong side and woven in as required by the pattern. This creates double-thick, dense, durable, and warm fabric ideally suited for knitting to protect against the harsh, cold, and damp climate of Scandinavia and the Nordic countries. And of course, garments made in this technique are traditionally made from the most abundant and readily available of natural materials—wool!

These techniques have been used in the following projects: Mootie Fair Isle Socks (see page 20), Ida Icelandic Lace & Patterned Mitts (see page 30), Åsa Mittens (see page 36), Oda Baby Blanket (see page 54), Annelli Doll (see page 58), Liisi Open Cardigan (see page 64), Oluffa Doorstop (see page 76), Onni Child's Sweater and Hat (see page 88), and Tovio Mittens and Hat (see page 96).

Twined Knitting

Although conventional knitting was practiced, the vast majority of early Swedish knitting, especially in the northern areas, was in fact twined knitting: *Tvåändsstickat* or two-ended knitting. This technique, in which the knitter uses both ends of the same ball of yarn and then twists the two yarns after each stitch, produces a uniform fabric of double thickness that is smooth, firm, warm, and hard wearing.

This style of knitting is ideally suited to mitten and sock

Liisi Open Cardigan (see page 64) features delicate colorwork on the shoulders and arms.

making. Less elastic than conventional knitting, twined knitting is an ideal base for embroidery; there are many examples of beautiful, brightly embroidered twined knitted mittens and gloves from the Dalarna area of Sweden. Extra time and effort was afforded to the making and decoration of mittens for festive and special occasions. These were not only heavily embroidered with various stylized flowers, leaves, and hearts, but also had colorful tufted borders and edgings. Crook stitches, distinctive raised patterning effects achieved only with twined knitting, were used as decoration, either in conjunction with embroidery or on their own.

These techniques have been used in the following projects: Birta Twined Hat (see page 42), Freja Twined Scarf (see page 46), and Nanna Twined Mitts (see page 50).

Traditional Nordic Yarns

Nanna Twined Mitts (see page 50) are thick and durable: a hallmark of twined knitting.

Because the projects in this book use traditional knitting techniques, I used authentically Nordic high-quality natural wool yarns from sustainable sources to create wearable contemporary garments and gifts. If these yarns are not readily available to you, you can consult the Materials list within each project to find the requirements for an appropriate substitution.

All the yarns used in this book are made from 100% pure wool. Many are from small sustainable suppliers using indigenous sheep breeds; others are from manufacturers with a long history. All of these natural-fiber wool yarns are very special indeed. Knitting with wool yarns that have been used for centuries will not only connect us with past traditions, but will also make beautiful long-lasting projects.

You can read more about the unique qualities of these individual yarns on page 123.

Suppliers listed for these yarns are listed on page 126, and again, information is provided in the pattern so that you can easily make substitutions.

Freja Twined Scarf (see page 46) is made using twined knitting, in which the inner and outer ends of the yarn ball are knit concurrently.

Patterns

Dimitie Scarf

SHETLAND ISLANDS

Lace knitting in Shetland probably long predates colored, patterned knitting. There is a wealth of traditional Shetland lace-knitting techniques, evident in the archive collections in the Shetland Museum (www.shetland-museum.org.uk). The geographic position of Shetland far out in the Atlantic Ocean ensured inclusion in an ancient trade route that stretched from the neighboring Faroe Islands, Scandinavia, and beyond to the Baltics. Shetland would have easily been exposed to an inspirational array of exotic textiles, handicrafts, and knitted lace from these countries and from even as far away as Spain. Patterns and stitches would have been copied, adapted, learned by heart, and passed from generation to generation.

The most exquisite, magnificently patterned knitted lace shawls were traditionally made on Unst, the most northerly of the Shetland Islands. These shawls were so cobweb-fine they could be passed through a wedding ring. The Shetland Hap shawls, however, used less intricate lace designs and were knitted in natural shades for everyday wear. This little Dimitie Scarf uses traditional lace borders, Christmas tree motifs, and the classic Grand Picot Eyelet lace stitch, which is reversible.

FINISHED SIZE
3½" (9 cm) wide by 73" (185.5 cm) long.

YARN
Laceweight (#1 Super Fine).

Shown here: Jamieson & Smith 2-ply Lace Yarn (100% wool; 185 yd [169 m]/25 g): #L1A natural white, 2 balls.

NEEDLES
Size U.S. 2 (2.75 mm) knitting needles. Adjust needle size if necessary to obtain the correct gauge.

NOTIONS
Stitch holder, tapestry needle.

GAUGE
36 sts and 22 rows = 4" (10 cm) over Grand Picot Eyelet patt.

Stitch Guide

Lace Border

Row 1 and all other odd-numbered rows: Knit.

Row 2: K4, yo, (knit into front, back, then front) of next st, (turn, k3) twice, (sl 2nd st over the last st and off needle) twice—6 sts.

Row 4: K5, yo, (knit into front, back, then front) of next st, (turn, k3) twice, (sl 2nd st over the last st and off needle) twice—7 sts.

Row 6: K6, yo, (knit into front, back, then front) of next st, (turn, k3) twice, (sl 2nd st over the last st and off needle) twice—8 sts.

Row 8: K7, yo, (knit into front, back, then front) of next st, (turn, k3) twice, (sl 2nd st over the last st and off needle) twice—9 sts.

Row 10: K8, yo, (knit into front, back, then front) of next st, (turn, k3) twice, (sl 2nd st over the last st and off needle) twice—10 sts.

Row 12: K9, (knit into front, back, then front) of next st, (turn, k3) twice, (sl 2nd st over the last st and off needle) twice—10 sts.

Row 14: K7, skp, (knit into front, back, then front) of next st, (turn, k3) twice, (sl 2nd st over the last st and off needle) twice—9 sts.

Row 16: K6, skp, (knit into front, back, then front) of next st, (turn, k3) twice, (sl 2nd st over the last st and off needle) twice—8 sts.

Row 18: K5, skp, (knit into front, back, then front) of next st, (turn, k3) twice, (sl 2nd st over the last st and off needle) twice—7 sts.

Row 20: K4, skp, (knit into front, back, then front) of next st, (turn, k3) twice, (sl 2nd st over the last st and off needle) twice—6 sts.

Row 22: K3, skp, (knit into front, back, then front) of next st, (turn, k3) twice, (sl 2nd st over the last st and off needle) twice—5 sts.

Row 23: Knit.

Rep Rows 2–23 for patt.

Grand Picot Eyelet

(multiple of 3 plus 4 edge sts)

Row 1: K2, *sk2p, (yo) twice; rep from * to last 2 sts, k2.

Row 2: K2, *(p1, k1) into the double yo, p1; rep from * to last 2 sts, k2.

Row 3: Knit.

Rep Rows 1–3 for patt.

Lace

(multiple of 16 sts plus 5)

Row 1 and all other WS rows: K2, purl to last 2 sts, k2.

Row 2: K3, *k5, k2tog, yo, k1, yo, ssk, k6; rep from * to last 2 sts, k2.

Row 4: K3, *k4, k2tog, yo, k3, yo, ssk, k5; rep from * to last 2 sts, k2.

Row 6: K3, *k3, (k2tog, yo) twice, k1, (yo, ssk) twice, k4; rep from * to last 2 sts, k2.

Row 8: K3, *k2, (k2tog, yo) twice, k3, (yo, ssk) twice, k3; rep from * to last 2 sts, k2.

Row 10: K3, *k1, (k2tog, yo) 3 times, k1, (yo, ssk) 3 times, k2; rep from * to last 2 sts, k2.

Row 12: Rep Row 4.

Row 14: Rep Row 6.

Row 16: Rep Row 4.

Row 18: Rep Row 6.

Row 20: Rep Row 8.

Row 22: Rep Row 6.

Row 24: Rep Row 4.

Row 26: Rep Row 2.

Row 28: K3, *k6, k2tog, yo, k8; rep from * to last 2 sts, k2.

Row 29: Rep Row 1.

SCARF

CO 5 sts. Work Rows 1–23 of Lace Border patt, then rep Rows 2–23 two more times. BO.

With RS of facing, pick up and knit 37 sts along straight edge.

Next row (WS): Knit.

Work Rows 1–3 of Grand Picot Eyelet patt.

Next row: Knit.

Work Rows 1–29 of Lace patt.

Next row (dec): K2, p1, p2tog, p13, p2tog, p12, p2tog, p1, k2—34 sts rem.

Next row (dec): K2, k1, (ssk, k11) twice, ssk, k3—31 sts rem.

Work Rows 1–3 of Grand Picot Eyelet patt. 106 times, then work Rows 1 and 2 once more; piece should measure about 36½" (92.5 cm). Place sts on holder.

Make the other half of the scarf same as first half.

FINISHING

Place held sts back on needle. With RS facing and both needles next to each other, graft pieces tog using Kitchener st.

Weave in ends.

Handwash in warm soapy water and carefully roll up in a towel and gently squeeze out excess water.

Reshape without pinning and leave to dry flat away from sun or heat source.

Press very lightly with a warm iron over a damp cloth.

Mootie Fair Isle Socks

SHETLAND ISLANDS

Inspiration for the Mootie socks came from the many beautifully colored and patterned traditional Fair Isle socks that are kept in the archives of the Shetland museum (www.shetland-museum.org.uk). The museum holds lovely examples of long socks knitted with allover motifs in tones of blue, gray, pink, and the deepest beetroot red, as well as traditional golfing stockings from the 1920s, knitted in natural tones with elaborately patterned cuffs.

The Mootie socks are designed with the classic Shetland stylized Tree of Life—a motif that universally represents the spring, fertility, and growth, and also symbolizes the connection between the living world and the underworld. The ornate pattern lends itself beautifully to using gradating shades of yarn, as does the classic Shetland zigzag pattern that is incorporated just above the ankle.

The socks are knitted in the round using the Fair Isle technique for the color pattern with a simple lace pattern and lace border for the cuff. The yarn is also stranded, or carried, over the plain parts of the knitting, making the socks consistently double thick and therefore superbly warm and comfortable.

FINISHED MEASUREMENTS
7¾" (19.5 cm) foot circumference and 9¾" (25 cm) long.

YARN
Fingering weight (#1 Super Fine).

Shown here: Jamieson & Smith 2-ply Jumper Weight (100% wool; 125 yd [115 m]/25 g): 2 balls each #FC34 blue (A) and #80 dark brown (J); 1 ball each #118 green (B), #202 natural (C), #75 turquoise (D), #FC7 light orange (E), #125 dark orange (F), #93 scarlet (G), #1403 deep red (H), and #9113 beetroot red (I).

NEEDLES
Size U.S. 2 (2.75 mm) needles: straight and double-pointed (dpn). Adjust needle sizes if necessary to obtain the correct gauge.

NOTIONS
Marker (m), tapestry needle.

GAUGE
30 sts and 36 rnd = 4" (10 cm) in leg chart worked in rounds.

Stitch Guide

Jogless Join

Pick up the first stitch from the previous round and place it on the left needle next to the first stitch of the next round and knit this picked up stitch and first stitch of the next round together.

Use this technique whenever knitting patterned rounds and when decreasing in pattern.

NOTES   Work "skp" to decrease at the beginning of rounds and "ssk" at the end of rounds. Where the first stitch at the beginning of rounds is a colored stitch, use the jogless-join technique and k2tog instead of skp.

SOCKS

Border

With straight needles and A, CO 7 sts.

Work Rows 1–4 repeat of Lace Border chart 27 times; piece should measure about 11¾" (30 cm) and should stretch to about 13½"–14" (34.5–35.5 cm).

BO rem 7 sts.

Leg

With dpn and A, pick up and knit 73 sts along straight edge of border.

Distribute sts over 4 dpn with 19 sts on Needle 1 and 18 sts each on Needles 2, 3, and 4. Place marker (pm) for beg of rnd and join for working in rnds.

Work Rnds 1–12 of Lace Leaf chart.

Next (dec) rnd: K2tog, knit to end—72 sts.

Work Rnds 1–60 of Leg chart and dec at beg and end of Rnds

21, 25, 29, and 33—64 sts rem. Distribute sts with 16 sts on each needle. Cut B and join a 2nd strand of J.

Next rnd: *K2 with first strand of J, k2 with 2nd strand of J; rep from * around.

Heel

Cont with 2 strands of J.

Row 1: K16, turn.

Row 2 (WS): Sl 1, p31, turn; leave rem 32 sts on separate dpn. Cont back and forth on the 32 heel sts.

Row 3 (RS): *Sl 1, k1; rep from * across.

Row 4 (WS): *Sl 1, purl to end.

Rep Rows 3 and 4 fifteen more times; heel should measure about 2¾" (7 cm).

Shape Heel

Row 1: K18 sts, skp, k1, turn.

Row 2: Sl 1, p5, p2tog, p1, turn.

Row 3: Sl 1, k6, skp, k1, turn.

Row 4: Sl 1, p7, p2tog, p1, turn.

Row 5: Sl 1, k8, skp, k1, turn.

Row 6: Sl 1, p9, p2tog, p1, turn.

Row 7: Sl 1, k10, skp, k1, turn.

Row 8: Sl 1, p11, p2tog, p1, turn.

Row 9: Sl 1, k12, skp, k1, turn.

Row 10: Sl 1, p13, p2tog, p1, turn.

Row 11: Sl 1, k14, skp, k1, turn.

Row 12: Sl 1, p15, p2tog, p1, turn.

Row 13: Sl 1, k16, skp, turn,

Row 14: Sl 1, p16, p2tog, turn—18 sts rem.

Row 15: K9.

Lace Border

Lace Leaf

beg

- ☐ k on RS, p on WS
- • p on RS, k on WS
- ☐ o yo
- ☐ / k2tog on RS
- ☐ ⟍ k2tog on WS
- ☐ ⋌ sk2p
- ⌒ bind off 1 st
- ☐ end last rep ssk
- ☐ pattern repeat

Gusset

Cont with 2 strands of J. Using dpn, Needle 1, knit rem 9 heel sts, pick up and knit 16 sts along edge of heel; Needles 2 and 3, knit across the held 32 instep sts; Needle 4, pick up and knit 16 sts along rem edge of heel, knit the rem 9 heel sts—82 sts.

Distribute sts if necessary with 25 sts (9 heel sts and 16 gusset sts) each on Needles 1 and 4 and 16 instep sts each on Needles 2 and 3. Pm for beg of rnd and join for working in rnds; rnds start at back of heel.

Next (dec) rnd: Needle 1, knit to last 3 sts, k2tog, k1; Needles 2 and 3, knit; Needle 4, k1, ssk, knit to end—2 sts dec'd.

Next rnd: *K2 with first strand of J, k2 with 2nd strand of J; rep from * around.

Rep last 2 rnds 8 more times—64 sts rem; 16 sts on each needle.

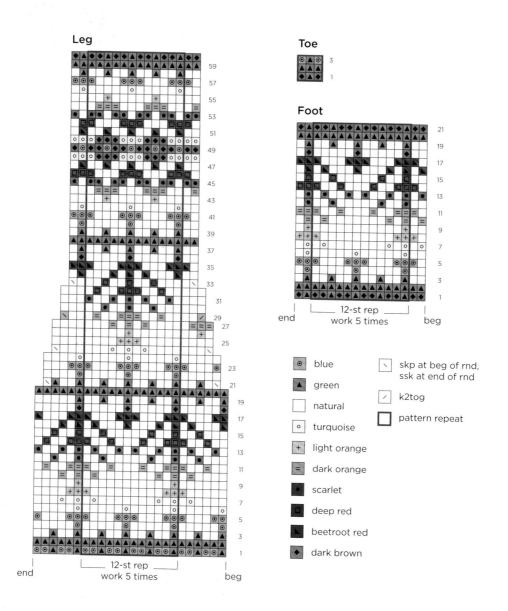

Leg

59
57
55
53
51
49
47
45
43
41
39
37
35
33
31
29
27
25
23
21
19
17
15
13
11
9
7
5
3
1

end

12-st rep
work 5 times

beg

Toe

3
1

Foot

21
19
17
15
13
11
9
7
5
3
1

end

12-st rep
work 5 times

beg

⊙ blue

▲ green

☐ natural

∘ turquoise

+ light orange

= dark orange

● scarlet

▣ deep red

◣ beetroot red

◆ dark brown

\ skp at beg of rnd,
  ssk at end of rnd

/ k2tog

☐ pattern repeat

Foot

Work 3 rnds even.

Cut 1 strand of J and join B. Work Rows 1–21 of Foot chart. Cut B and join a 2nd strand of J.

Work 3 rnds even; foot should measure about 6¼" (16 cm) from heel.

Shape Toe

Next (dec) rnd: *K6, k2tog; rep from * around—8 sts dec'd.

Work 6 rnds even.

Next (dec) rnd: *K5, k2tog; rep from * around—8 sts dec'd.

Cut 1 strand of J and join B. Work Rows 1–3 of Toe chart. Cut J and join 2nd strand of A. Work 2 rnds even.

Next (dec) rnd: *K4, k2tog; rep from * around—8 sts dec'd.

Work 4 rnds even.

Next (dec) rnd: *K3, k2tog; rep from * around—8 sts dec'd.

Work 3 rnds even.

Next (dec) rnd: *K2, k2tog; rep from * around—8 sts dec'd.

Work 2 rnds even.

Next (dec) rnd: *K1, k2tog; rep from * around—8 sts dec'd.

Work 1 rnd even.

Next (dec) rnd: *K2tog; rep from * around—8 sts rem.

Cut yarn, leaving an 8" (20.5 cm) tail, thread tail through rem sts, pull tight to close hole, and fasten off on WS.

FINISHING

Weave in all ends.

Handwash in warm soapy water and carefully roll up in a towel and gently squeeze out excess water. Reshape without pinning or stretching and leave to dry flat away from sun or direct heat.

Press very lightly with a warm iron over a damp cloth.

Fridmar Hat

ICELAND

The Fridmar Hat design is based on the classic bag caps or stocking caps that were traditionally knitted in all Scandinavian and northern countries. These caps would have been exceptionally warm as they were knitted in the round, in one piece, with one end simply pushed up inside the other to create a fantastically thick and insulating double-lined cap.

The caps were often decorated with bands of colored traditional and symbolic motifs such as stylized stars, squares, and zigzags. This type of patterning, which requires a stranded or Fair Isle technique to knit, would have created a double thick fabric and consequently would have provided even more insulation.

The Fridmar Hat is designed in exactly the same way as the traditional Scandinavian caps and will appeal to both men and women. It is knitted in a superbly warm pre-spun yarn that creates a soft, light, and lofty insulating fabric. But instead of using colored motifs as decoration, it has simple textured stitches. These create a slightly ribbed pattern and border, ensuring a snug, comfortable fit.

FINISHED SIZE
Circumference 29½" (75 cm).

YARN
Worsted weight (#4 Medium).

Shown here: Ístex Plötulopi (100% wool; 328 yd [300 m]/3½ oz [100 g]): #1027 light ash heather, 1 skein.

This yarn is very delicate and must be handled with care when knitting; be careful not to pull the yarn too hard and break it.

NEEDLES
Set of 5 size U.S. 7 (4.5 mm) double-pointed (dpn). Adjust needle size if necessary to obtain the correct gauge.

NOTIONS
Marker (m), tapestry needle.

GAUGE
16 sts and 25 rnds = 4" (10 cm) over main patt.

Stitch Guide

Main Pattern

(multiple of 3 sts)

Rnd 1: *K1, knit next st and leave it on needle, purl the same st and next st tog; rep from *.

Rnd 2: Knit.

Rep Rnds 1 and 2 for patt.

Border Pattern

(multiple of 3 sts)

Rnd 1: *K1, k1-b; rep from *.

Rnd 2: Knit.

Rep Rnds 1 and 2 for patt.

HAT

Lining

CO 8 sts. Divide sts evenly over 4 dpn. Place marker (pm) and join for working in rnds.

Rnd 1 and all other odd-number rnds: Knit.

Rnd 2 (inc): *K1f&b; rep from * around—16 sts.

Rnd 4: *K1, k1f&b; rep from * around—24 sts.

Rnd 6: *K2, k1f&b; rep from * around—32 sts.

Rnd 8: *K3, k1f&b; rep from * around—40 sts.

Rnd 10: *K4, k1f&b; rep from * around—48 sts.

Rnd 12: *K5, k1f&b; rep from * around—56 sts.

Rnd 14: *K6, k1f&b; rep from * around—64 sts.

Rnd 16: *K7, k1f&b; rep from * around—72 sts.

Rnd 18: *K8, k1-b, (k8, k1f&b) 3 times; rep from * once more—78 sts.

Rnd 19: Knit.

Work Rnds 1 and 2 of Main patt 21 times; piece should measure about 9" (23 cm) from CO, ending with Rnd 2.

Brim

Work Rnds 1 and 2 of Border patt 5 times; piece should measure about 11½" (29 cm) from CO.

Work Rnds 1 and 2 of Main patt 15 times; piece should measure about 15¼" (39 cm) from CO (it should be just a little longer than the lining when folded at beg of Border patt.

Weave in ends.

Crown

Rnd 1 (dec): *K8, k1-b, (k8, ssk) 3 times; rep from * once more—72 sts.

Rnd 2 and all other even-number rnds: Knit.

Rnd 3: *K7, ssk; rep from * around—64 sts.

Rnd 5: *K6, ssk; rep from * around—56 sts.

Rnd 7: *K5, ssk; rep from * around—48 sts.

Rnd 9: *K4, ssk; rep from * around—40 sts.

Rnd 11: *K3, ssk; rep from * around—32 sts.

Rnd 13: *K2, ssk; rep from * around—24 sts.

Rnd 15: *K1, ssk; rep from * around—16 sts.

Rnd 17: *Ssk; rep from * around—8 sts.

Cut yarn, leaving an 8" (20.5 cm) tail, thread through rem sts, carefully pull tight to close hole, fasten off on WS.

FINISHING

Fold lining to inside of hat. Carefully secure yarn ends from CO and end to secure the two crowns tog.

Handwash in warm soapy water and very carefully roll up in a towel and gently squeeze out excess water.

Reshape and leave to dry flat away from sun or heat source.

Ida Icelandic Lace and Patterned Mitts

ICELAND

Iceland has a long history of narrative embroideries, and the birds decorating the Ida Mitts were inspired by those on the *Riddarateppid,* a woven Icelandic bed-cover hundreds of years old that now resides in the National Museum of Iceland in Reykjavik (www.thjodminjasafn.is/english). This coverlet is embellished entirely in long-armed stitch, an embroidery stitch similar to cross-stitch but much more hard wearing. It is decorated with stylized humans, horses, entwined foliage, birds, and beasts. In Icelandic folklore, birds were considered to be symbols of protection and

good luck; they were linked to the spirit world and were believed to be able to carry souls to the afterlife, where they then also became birds. Traditionally, birds were often used to decorate mittens and gloves as protection for the wearer.

The simple lace pattern is highlighted by the movement from light to dark natural shades of Icelandic fleece. This technique has been traditionally used to symbolize light to dark, day to night, summer to winter.

FINISHED MEASUREMENTS

7¼" (18.5 cm) hand circumference and 10¼" (26 cm) long.

YARN

Laceweight (#1 Super Fine).

Shown here: Ístex Lodband Einband (100% wool: 246 yd [225 m]/50 g): #0851 white (A), 2 skeins; #1026 ash heather (B), 1 skein; #0886 beige heather (C), 1 skein; #0885 oatmeal heather (D), 1 skein; #0867 chocolate (E), 1 skein; #0852 black sheep heather (F), 1 skein.

NEEDLES

Set of 5 size 2.5 mm (no exact U.S. equivalent; between U.S. sizes 1 and 2) double-pointed needles (dpn). Adjust needle size if necessary to obtain the correct gauge.

NOTIONS

Markers (m), holder or waste yarn, tapestry needle.

GAUGE

31 sts and 37 rnds = 4" (10 cm) in color chart worked in rounds.

30 sts and 39 rnds = 4" (10 cm) in lace patt worked in rounds.

Stitch Guide

Lace

(multiple of 12 sts)

Row 1: *P1, k5; rep from *.

Row 2: *P1, k2tog, k3, yo, p1, yo, k3, ssk; rep from *.

Jogless Join

Pick up the first stitch from the previous round and place it on the left needle next to the first stitch of the next round and knit this picked up stitch and first stitch of the next round together.

Use this technique whenever knitting color patterned rounds and when decreasing in pattern.

RIGHT MITT

With A, CO 48 sts. Distribute sts evenly over 4 dpn with 12 sts on each needle. Place marker (pm) for beg of rnd and join for working in rnds.

Working Rnds 1 and 2 of Lace chart 3 times (6 rnds total) for each color, work stripes as foll: A, B, C, D, E, F, E, D, C, B, then A. Piece should measure about 6¾" (17 cm) from beg.

Inc rnd 1: With A, *k1b&f, k10, k1f&b; rep from * 3 more times—56 sts.

Inc rnd 2: *K1b&f, knit to end of needle; rep from * 3 more times—60 sts.

Rearrange sts with 17 sts on Needle 1, 16 sts on Needle 2, 14 sts on Needle 3, and 13 sts on Needle 4.

Work Rows 1–4 of Hand chart, beg rnds for Right Mitt.

Thumb Gusset

Next rnd Work Row 5 of chart over 34 sts, pm, k1f&b and pm between sts, work to end of rnd—1 st inc'd for beg of thumb gusset (Row 1 of Right Thumb chart).

Next rnd: Work Row 6 of Hand chart to m, sm, k1f&b (Row 2 of Right Thumb chart), sm, work to end of rnd—1 st inc'd.

Cont through Row 19 of Hand chart and Row 15 of Right Thumb chart—71 sts; 60 sts for hand, and 11 sts for thumb gusset.

Next rnd: Work Row 20 of Hand chart over first 34 sts, place next 18 sts on holder or waste yarn for thumb, CO 7 sts over hole, work as established to end—60 sts.

Work Rows 21–27 of Hand chart as established.

With A, knit 1 rnd. Rearrange sts with 17 sts on Needle 1, 14 sts on Needle 2, 17 sts on Needle 3, and 12 sts on Needle 4.

Work Rows 1 and 2 of Lace chart 3 times. BO all sts kwise.

Thumb

Place 18 sts from holder on dpn, pick up and knit 8 sts along CO sts above thumb opening—26 sts. Distribute sts over 4 dpn with 8 sts each on Needles 1 and 3 and 9 sts each over Needles 2 and 4. Pm for beg of rnd and join for working in rnds.

Work Rows 16–24 of Right Thumb chart.

Next (dec) rnd: K6, k2tog, k12, ssk, knit to end—24 sts rem. Rearrange sts if necessary with 6 sts on each needle.

Work Rows 1 and 2 of Lace chart 3 times. BO all sts kwise.

LEFT MITT

Work left mitt same as right through Inc rnd 2—60 sts.

Rearrange sts with 14 sts on Needle 1, 13 sts on Needle 2, 16 sts on Needle 3, and 17 sts on Needle 4.

Work Rows 1–4 of Hand chart, beg rnds for Left Mitt.

Thumb Gusset

Next rnd: Work Row 5 of chart over 25 sts, pm, k1f&b and pm between sts, work to end of rnd—1 st inc'd for beg of thumb gusset (Row 1 of Right Thumb chart).

Next rnd: Work Row 6 of Hand chart to m, sm, k1f&b (Row 2 of Right Thumb chart), sm, work to end of rnd—1 st inc'd.

Cont through Row 19 of Hand chart and Row 15 of Left Thumb chart—71 sts; 60 sts for hand, and 11 sts for thumb gusset.

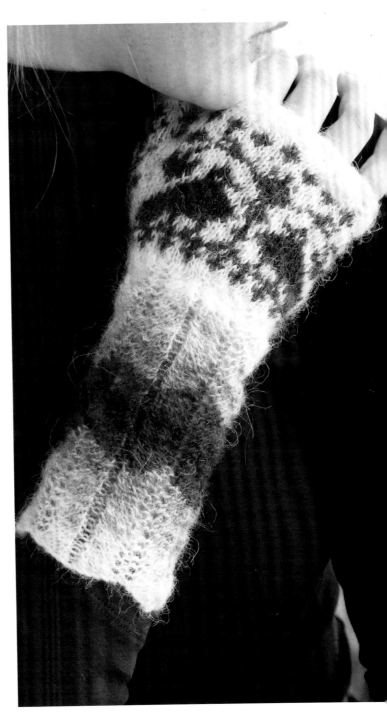

Hand

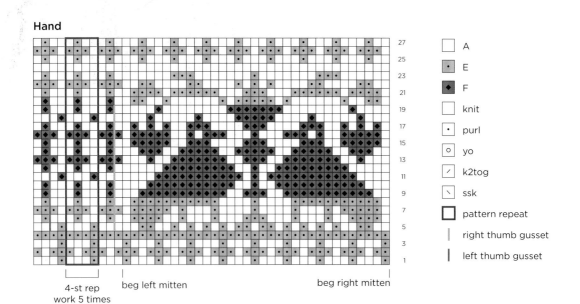

27
25
23
21
19
17
15
13
11
9
7
5
3
1

	A
▨	E
◆	F
	knit
•	purl
○	yo
╱	k2tog
╲	ssk
▢	pattern repeat
│	right thumb gusset
▌	left thumb gusset

4-st rep
work 5 times

beg left mitten

beg right mitten

Left Thumb

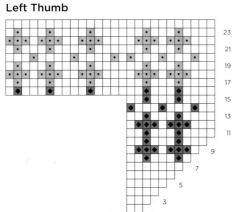

23
21
19
17
15
13
11
9
7
5
3

Right Thumb

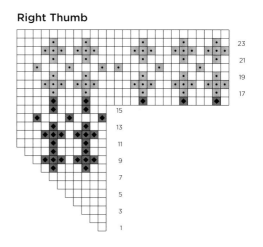

23
21
19
17
15
13
11
9
7
5
3
1

Lace

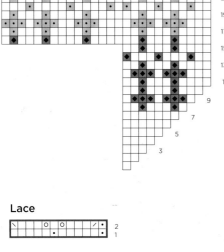

| ╲ | | ○ | ○ | | ╱ | • | 2 |
| | | | • | | | | 1 |

Next rnd: Work Row 20 of Hand chart over first 19 sts, place next 18 sts on holder or waste yarn for thumb, CO 7 sts over hole, work as established to end—60 sts.

Work Rows 21–27 of Hand chart as established.

With A, knit 1 rnd. Rearrange sts with 17 sts on Needle 1, 14 sts on Needle 2, 17 sts on Needle 3, and 12 sts on Needle 4.

Work Rows 1 and 2 of Lace chart 3 times. BO all sts kwise.

Thumb

Place 18 sts from holder on dpn, pick up and knit 8 sts along CO sts above thumb opening—26 sts. Distribute sts over 4 dpn with 8 sts each on Needles 1 and 3 and 9 sts each over Needles 2 and 4. Pm for beg of rnd and join for working in rnds.

Work Rows 16–24 of Left Thumb chart.

Next (dec) rnd: K6, k2tog, k12, ssk, knit to end—24 sts rem. Rearrange sts if necessary with 6 sts on each needle.

Work Rows 1 and 2 of Lace chart 3 times. BO all sts kwise.

FINISHING

Weave in all ends.

Handwash in warm soapy water and very carefully roll up in a towel and gently squeeze out excess water. Reshape and leave to dry flat away from sun or heat source.

Press very lightly with a warm iron over a damp cloth.

Åsa Mittens

SWEDEN

Inspired by the traditional folk mittens and gloves kept in the Nordiska Museet in Stockholm (www .nordiskamuseet.se), these simple Åsa Mittens are knitted in the round using the stranded knitting technique. They have peasant thumbs (thumbs on the palm side) and are embroidered with single French knots, duplicate stitches, and cross-stitches. Many of the traditional Swedish mittens were highly decorated with colorful, intricately embroidered flowers, foliage, and stylized geometric borders and were finished with colorful tufted and embroidered bands. Others were much plainer, decorated with just a two-color geometric pattern with simple ribbed cuffs or no particular cuff at all.

The stylized foliage patterns on the Åsa mittens echo the ancient Tree of Life motif, one of the most sacred of all symbolic shapes in Norse mythology. The Norse Tree of Life represents the connection between the living world (light and sky) and the underworld (darkness and earth). It is also a motif associated with the springtime and the hope of rebirth and renewal.

Use a pure wool yarn—ideally one that, once washed, will felt slightly to create a good firm fabric.

FINISHED MEASUREMENTS

8½" (21.5 cm) hand circumference.

YARN

Sportweight (#2 Fine).

Shown here: Ullcentrum Oland 2-Thread Wool Yarn (100% wool; 328 yd [300 m]/100 g): light gray or petrol (A), 1 skein; white (B), 1 skein; yellow or red (C), small amount; red or yellow (D), small amount; petrol or yellow (E), small amount.

NEEDLES

Set of 5 size 3 mm (no exact U.S. equivalent; between U.S. sizes 2 and 3) double-pointed needles (dpn). Adjust needle size if necessary to obtain the correct gauge.

NOTIONS

Marker (m), holder or waste yarn, tapestry needle.

GAUGE

26 sts and 32 rnds = 4" (10 cm) in chart patt worked in rounds.

NOTE

Use the jogless join when working from the charts to create a smooth transition from one round to the next over the chart pattern.

⊡	A
☐	B
⟍	ssk
⟋	k2tog
○	knit with B, French knot with B
◉	knit with A, French knot with C
●	knit with B, French knot with E
V	knit with B, duplicate st with D
X	large cross-st with C
—	right thumb opening
—	left thumb opening

Stitch Guide

Jogless Join

Pick up the first stitch from the previous round and place it on the left needle next to the first stitch of the next round and knit this picked up stitch and first stitch of the next round together.

Use this technique whenever knitting patterned rounds and when decreasing in pattern.

RIGHT MITTEN

With A, CO 60 sts. Distribute sts evenly over 4 dpn (15 sts on each needle). Place marker (pm) for beg of rnd and join for working in rnds.

Rnd 1: Knit.

Rnds 2–4: Purl.

Rnds 5–6: Knit.

Work Hand chart, beg where marked for Right Mitten, work 44 sts, work first 16 sts of chart to complete rnd. Cont as established through Rnd 21.

Rnds 22 and 23: Ssk, work as established to end of Needle 2, ssk, work to end of rnd—56 sts. Rearrange sts with 14 sts on each needle.

Cont through chart Row 39.

Hand

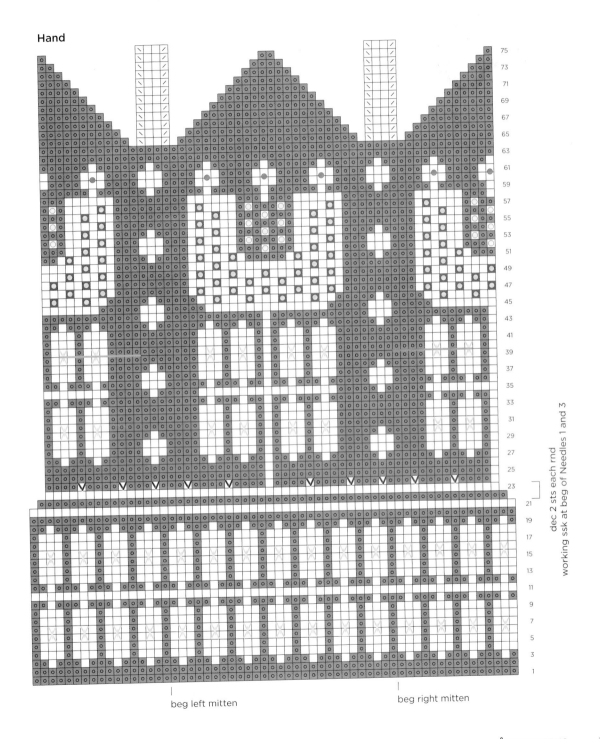

Left Thumb

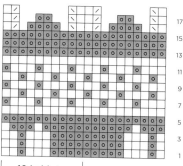

17
15
13
11
9
7
5
3
1

└─10 held sts─┘
for thumb opening

Right Thumb

17
15
13
11
9
7
5
3
1

└─10 held sts─┘
for thumb opening

⊙	A
☐	B
◥	ssk
◢	k2tog
⊙	knit with B, French knot with B
⊙	knit with A, French knot with C
⊙	knit with B, French knot with E
V	knit with B, duplicate st with D
✕	large cross-st with C
—	right thumb opening
—	left thumb opening

Thumbhole

Rnd 40: Needles 1 and 2, work as established; Needle 3, work 3 sts, place next 10 sts on holder or waste yarn, CO 10 sts using backward-loop method, work to end of rnd.

Cont through chart Row 64.

Shaping the Top of the Mitten

Arrange sts if necessary with 14 sts on each needle.

Shape top foll Rows 65–76 of chart—8 sts rem.

Cut yarn, leaving an 8″ (20.5 cm) tail, thread tail through rem sts, pull tight to close hole, and fasten off on WS.

Thumb

Return 10 held thumb sts to dpn, pick up and knit 10 sts along the CO sts above the opening foll colors in Right Thumb chart—20 sts. Pm for beg of rnd and join for working in rnds.

Work Rnds 1–18 of Right Thumb chart—8 sts rem.

Cut yarn, leaving an 8″ (20.5 cm) tail, thread tail through rem sts, pull tight to close hole, and fasten off on WS.

LEFT MITTEN

Work left mitten same as right mitten through chart Row 39.

Thumbhole

Rnd 40: Needle 1, work as established; Needle 2, work 4 sts, place next 10 sts on holder or waste yarn, CO 10 sts using backward-loop method, work to end of rnd.

Cont same as right mitten.

FINISHING

Weave in ends.

Embroider mittens foll chart.

Handwash in warm soapy water and carefully roll up in a towel and gently squeeze out excess water. Reshape and leave to dry flat away from direct sun or heat source.

Press very lightly with a warm iron over a damp cloth.

Birta Twined Hat

SWEDEN

Red knitted woolen caps with either large or small tassels were worn by men as part of traditional Swedish folk costume in many regions of Sweden, most notably in Hälsingland, Halland, and Södermanland. The color red has long associations in folklore with magic protective qualities and would usually have been used to symbolize the sun, life, fire, and of course, blood, death, and sacrifice. These red knitted caps probably would have been worn both as a way of protection against any evil and as part of a "Sunday best" or special celebratory costume.

The Birta hat has been knitted in the round using the twined knitting method (as no doubt the original caps were knitted) and decorated with simple flowerlike motifs whose origin would have been the traditional Nordic eight-point star, simple twined crook stitches, and embroidery stitches. Ideally, use a pure wool yarn that is strong enough to withstand the rigors of twined knitting.

FINISHED SIZE
19" (48.5 cm) circumference.

YARN
Sportweight (#2 Fine).

Shown here: Ullcentrum Oland 2-Thread Wool Yarn (100% wool; 328 yd [300 m]/100 g): red (A); 1 skein; white (B), small amount; petrol (C), small amount.

NEEDLES
Set of 5 size 3 mm (no exact U.S. equivalent; between U.S. sizes 2 and 3) double-pointed needles (dpn). Adjust needle size if necessary to obtain the correct gauge.

NOTIONS
Marker (m), tapestry needle.

GAUGE
31½ sts and 32 rnds = 4" (10 cm) in twined stockinette worked in rounds.

Stitch Guide

Crook Stitch

(odd number of sts)

Join 2 strands of B: either strand can be chosen as the front strand for the first stitch of Rnd 1.

Rnd 1: With B, bring strand farthest right from right needle tip to front where it will rem throughout. P1 with front strand, *k1 with back strand, p1 with front strand; rep from *.

Bring front strand of B to back.

Rnd 2: With A, k1 with strand farthest from right needle tip. Bring strand that is now farthest from right needle tip to front where it will rem throughout. *P1 with front strand, k1 with back strand ; rep from *. Bring front strand of A to back.

Rnd 3: With B, rep Rnd 1.

Bring both strands of B to back and cut off B.

Rib

(multiple of 3 sts)

Row 1: *(P1, k1, p1) in crook st, k3; rep from *.

Row 2: *(K1, p1, k1) in crook st, k3; rep from *.

Rep Rnds 1 and 2 for patt.

Color Work

To work from chart, cut separate strands of white (B) for each motif and add the strand in as you continue to work twined stockinette with the two strands of red (A). Pick up B for use only in the area needed, always twisting the yarns being used, slipping the yarn onto a tapestry needle and threading it through to the back of each star pattern to return it to the correct position for the next round.

The contrast yarn does not need to be carried around the entire round but remains in the correct position ready for use.

HAT

With A, CO 150 sts using Twined Cast-On (see page 114). Distribute the sts evenly over 4 dpn with 38 sts each on Needles 1 and 3 and 37 sts each on Needles 2 and 4. Place marker (pm) for beg of rnd and join for working in rnds.

Work 22 rnds in Rib patt; piece should measure about 2¾" (7 cm) from beg.

Work 1 rnd in twined knitting (see page 121).

Ensure that all stitches are arranged evenly over the 4 needles (38, 37, 38, 37).

Next rnd (dec): Needle 1, k1, k2tog tbl, knit to last 3 sts, k2tog tfl, k1; Needle 2, knit to last 3 sts, k2tog tfl, k1; Needle 3, k1, k2tog tbl, knit to last 3 sts, k2tog tfl, k1; Needle 4, knit to last 3 sts, k2tog tfl, k1—144 sts rem; there should be 36 sts on each needle.

Work Rnds 1–9 of chart.

Work 2 rnds of twined knitting.

Shape Crown
Cont in twined knitting.

Next rnd (dec): *K7, ssk; rep from * around—128 sts rem.

Work 6 rnds even.

Next rnd (dec): *K6, ssk; rep from * around—112 sts rem.

Work 5 rnds even.

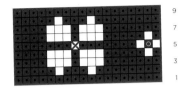

- · A
- □ B
- ⊙ k with A, French knot with C
- ☒ k with B, cross-st with C
- □ pattern repeat

Next rnd (dec): *K5, ssk; rep from * around—96 sts rem.

Work 4 rnds even.

Next rnd (dec): *K4, ssk; rep from * around—80 sts rem.

Work 3 rnds even.

Next rnd (dec): *K3, ssk; rep from * around—64 sts rem.

Work 2 rnds even.

Next rnd (dec): *K2, ssk; rep from * around—48 sts rem.

Work 1 rnd even.

Next rnd (rnd): *K1, ssk; rep from * around—32 sts rem.

Next rnd (dec): *Ssk; rep from * around—16 sts rem.

Cut yarn, leaving an 8″ (20.5 cm) tail, thread tail through rem sts, pull tight to close hole, fasten off on WS.

Finishing

With C, embroider French knots and cross-stitches foll chart.

With A, make a tassel and make a braid with 3 strands of yarn about 1½″ (3.8 cm), or desired length.

Attach the tassel to the braid, then secure rem end of braid to WS at top of hat.

Weave in ends.

Handwash in warm soapy water and carefully roll up in a towel and gently squeeze out excess water. Reshape and leave to dry flat away from sun or direct heat.

Press lightly with a warm iron over a damp cloth.

Freja Twined Scarf

SWEDEN

The deceptively simple two-color pattern on this classic long scarf was inspired by ancient Swedish weaving techniques known as *rosengång* (or rosepath) and monk's belt. These were names given to simple woven fabrics with many and varied geometric bands and allover patterns traditionally made with linen and wool. These fabrics were usually used as coverlets, and the geometric patterns would be repeated with subtle changes, often alternating the background and foreground colors to create extra variation.

Very similar simple two-color patterns were also found on early examples of twined mitts from Dalarna. These two-stitch repeat patterns are eminently suitable to twined knitting (which uses both outer and inner ends of the same ball of yarn at the same time) as you can divide your ball of yarn into two separate colors by winding the first half of the ball in one color and the second half in a contrasting color. Then, when you start knitting, you will be using one end of each color; the pattern and twined knitting will work hand in hand.

FINISHED SIZE
4½″ (11.5 cm) wide by 94″ (239 cm) long.

YARN
Sportweight (#2 Fine).

Shown here: Ullcentrum Oland 2-Thread Wool Yarn (100% wool; 328 yd [300 m]/100 g): red (A), 2 skeins; white (B), 2 skeins.

When preparing the yarn wind 100 g of white and then continue with 100 g of red (200 g ball). I also recommend preparing a small ball of White for knitting the plain white rnds of the pattern.

NEEDLES
Set of 5 size 3 mm (no exact U.S. equivalent; between U.S. sizes 2 and 3) double-pointed needles (dpn). Adjust needle size if necessary to obtain the correct gauge.

NOTIONS
Marker (m), tapestry needle.

GAUGE
32 sts and 29 rnds = 4″ (10 cm) over chart.

SCARF

*Using 1 strand of A and 2 strands of B, CO 60 sts using Twined Cast-On with Double Bead (see page 115). Divide sts evenly over 4 dpn (15 on each needle). Place marker (pm) and join for working in rnds.

Rnd 1: With B, work 1 rnd of twined purling (see page 121).

Rnd 2: With A, work 1 rnd of twined purling.*

Work chart as foll: Rnds 1–20 four times, Rnds 1–10 once, Rnds 21–74 once, Rnds 1–20 once, Rnds 1–10 once, Rnds 21–74 once, Rnds 1–20 once, (Rnds 21–74 once, Rnds 1–10 once) 2 times, (Rnds 21–74 once, Rnds 1–20 once) 2 times, Rnds 1–10 once, Rnds 21–74 once, Rnds 1–20 four times, Rnds 1–10 once. At the same time, when necessary to maintain alternating nature of pattern, shift beg of rnd on chart when starting a section of patt chart.

Note: On plain rnds, drop both strands from the 200 g ball, join B from the smaller ball and knit 1 rnd, cut this yarn, then cont with both strands from the 200 g ball.

When chart has been completed, BO kwise with A.

Edge

Rep from * to *. BO kwise with A.

Sew edge to BO edge of scarf using backstitch.

Finishing

Weave in ends.

With B, sew ends closed.

Handwash in warm soapy water and carefully roll up in a towel and gently squeeze out excess water. Reshape and leave to dry flat away from sun or direct heat.

Press lightly with a warm iron over a damp cloth.

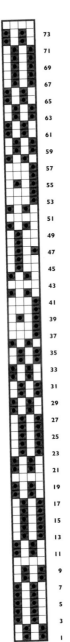

73
71
69
67
65
63
61
59
57
55
53
51
49
47
45
43
41
39
37
35
33
31
29
27
25
23
21
19
17
15
13
11
9
7
5
3
1

A

B

pattern repeat

Nanna Twined Mitts

NORWAY

Twined knitting has a very distinctive texture that is noticeably different from conventional knitting, and the back (or wrong side) of twined knitting has a unique quality and textural appeal. This is because as you knit with the two ends of the same ball of yarn, consistently using the back strand to form the new stitch, the back of the knitting will show a repetitive and even stranding of the two yarns; there is a beautifully ridged, almost honeycombed, texture to it. This firm yet slightly stretchy fabric is an ideal base for embroidery. Traditionally, twined mitts, mittens, and gloves would have been embroidered and decorated using both the wrong or the right side. Many were also given a fringed border as decoration, just like the one on these Nanna mitts; they were believed to give magical protection to the wearer, ensuring that the evil eye was suitably confused and therefore kept at bay.

I would recommend using a pure wool yarn that gives good stitch definition.

FINISHED MEASUREMENTS

8½" (21.5 cm) hand circumference and 7" (18 cm) long, excluding fringe.

YARN

Sportweight (#2 Fine).

Shown here: Dale of Norway Heilo (100% wool; 109 yd [100 m]/50 g): #0020 natural (MC), 2 balls; #0083 charcoal heather (A), 1 ball; #6642 light steel blue (B), 1 ball; only small amounts of A and B are needed.

NEEDLES

Set of 5 size 3 mm (no exact U.S. equivalent; between U.S. sizes 2 and 3) double-pointed needles (dpn). Adjust needle size if necessary to obtain the correct gauge.

NOTIONS

Marker (m), tapestry needle.

GAUGE

28 sts and 30 rnds = 4" (10 cm) in twined St st in rnds.

NOTE

Mitts are worked with the knit side of the twined St st showing but turned so the purl side becomes the right side of the finished mitt.

Thumb Gusset

Next (inc) rnd: Work as established to last 2 sts of Needle 2, knit into (back, then front) of next st, work to end—1 st inc'd.

Rep inc in same st every rnd 9 more times—70 sts.

Work 6 rnds even.

Next rnd: Needle 1, work as established; Needle 2, work first 7 sts, place next 18 sts onto holder, CO 8 sts over hole using backward-loop method, work to end—60 sts rem.

Knit 14 rnds even.

BO kwise, working ssk every 4th and 5th sts.

Thumb

Return 18 sts on hold to dpn, pick up and knit 8 sts along CO edge above thumb hole—26 sts. Pick up thumb sts carefully ensuring that the inside (which will be the RS of the finished mitt) looks neat. Arrange sts over 4 dpn with 7 sts each on Needles 1 and 3, and 6 sts each on Needles 2 and 4. Pm for beg of rnd and join for working in rnds.

Work 10 rnds twined knitting.

BO kwise, working ssk every 4th and 5th sts.

RIGHT MITT

Work right mitt same as left mitt through Rnd 20.

Thumb Gusset

Next (inc) rnd: Needles 1 and 2, work as established; Needle 3, k1, knit into (back, then front) of next st, work to end—1 st inc'd.

Rep inc in same st every rnd 9 more times—70 sts.

Work 6 rnds even.

Next rnd: Needles 1 and 2, work as established; Needle 3, place first 18 sts onto holder, CO 8 sts over hole, work to end—60 sts rem.

Cont right mitt same as left.

LEFT MITT

Using 3 strands of MC and Twined Cast-On with Double Bead (see page 115), CO 60 sts. Distribute sts evenly over 4 dpn (15 sts on each needle). Place marker (pm) for beg of rnd and join for working in rnds.

Rnds 1 and 2: Work 2 rnds twined purling (see page 121).

Rnds 3–16: Work 14 rnds twined knitting (see page 121).

Rnd 17: Rep Rnd 1.

Rnd 18: Rep Rnd 3.

Rnds 19 and 20: Rep last 2 rnds.

FINISHING

Turn mitts inside out so purl side is now the RS.

Embroider using cross-st and French knots using photo as guide.

Weave in all ends.

Fringe

Cut 80 strands of B, each 4" (10 cm) long. Using 4 strands at a time, thread strands from WS to RS at center of one st, *skip next st, thread ends through to WS in center of next st, thread next group of strands from WS to RS in center of next st; rep from * around.

With 1 strand of B threaded in tapestry needle, sew over the center of each group of strands on RS as foll: bring needle up from WS to RS at center of first group of strands, *pass needle back to WS, going over group of strands, pass needle somewhat loosely across WS to next group of strands, bring needle up from WS to RS at center of group of strands; rep from * around. Fasten off ends of yarn.

Rep with rem mitt.

Handwash in warm soapy water and carefully roll up in a towel and gently squeeze out excess water. Reshape and leave to dry flat away from sun or heat source.

Trim the fringe to about 1" (2.5 cm) long.

Press lightly with a warm iron over a damp cloth.

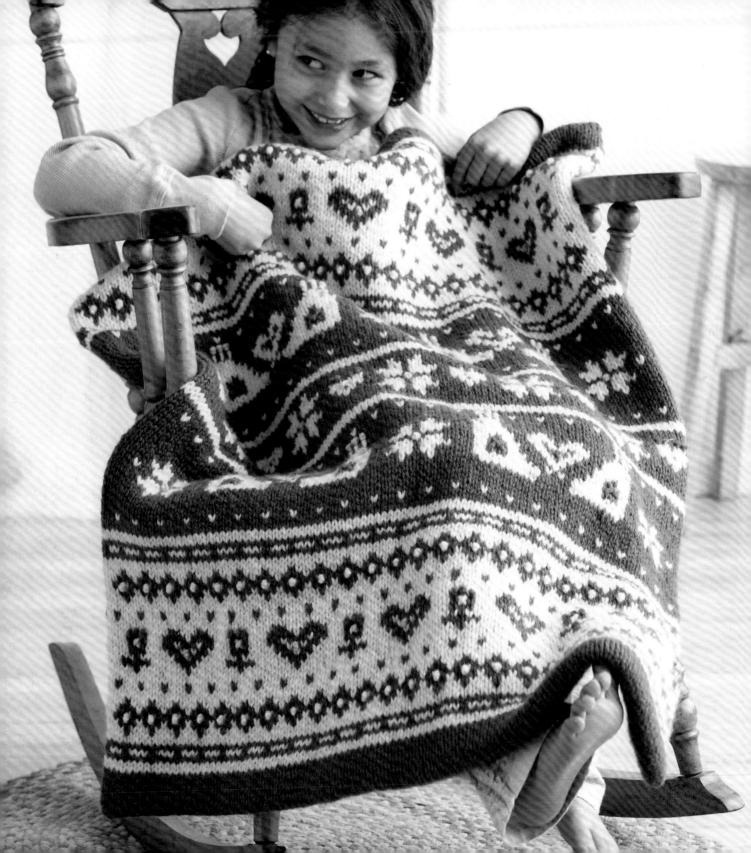

Oda Baby Blanket

NORWAY

Knitted in the round using the stranded knitting technique, the Oda Baby blanket is superbly warm and comforting. The blanket is decorated with folkloric patterns of ancient origin such as birds, hearts, stars, and flowers: all symbolic of protection and good luck. The stylized little bird and flower patterning were inspired by the now-famous pictorial Norwegian Selbu knitting, which was traditionally decorated with simple two-color stars, snowflakes, stylized reindeer, and other patterns that were adapted from handicrafts such as embroidery and weaving. The back of the blanket is also patterned with the traditional Norwegian *luse*, or lice, stitch that was used originally on the famous *lusekofte* jerseys from the southern valleys of Norway. These fine black wool jerseys were patterned all over with small white stitches and featured embroidered black fabric edgings and decorative buttons.

FINISHED SIZE
27" (68.5 cm) wide and 35½" (90 cm) long.

YARN
Chunky weight (#5 Bulky).

Shown here: Hillesvåg Ullvarefabrikk AS Hifa Trollgarn (100% wool; 124 yd [114 m]/3½ oz [100 g]): #757 soft brown (A), 7 skeins; #702 natural white (B), 5 skeins; #745 light blue (C), 1 skein; #743 light pink (D), 1 skein; #716 warm orange (E), 1 skein.

NEEDLES
Size U.S. 9 (5.5 mm): 32" (80) or longer circular (cir) needle. Adjust needle size if necessary to obtain the correct gauge.

NOTIONS
Markers (m), tapestry needle.

GAUGE
15 sts and 19 rows = 4" (10 cm) over chart patt worked in rounds.

Chart I

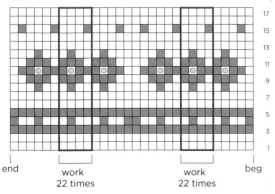

end   work 22 times   work 22 times   beg

17
15
13
11
9
7
5
3
1

Chart II

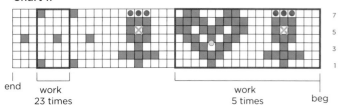

end   work 23 times   work 5 times   beg

7
5
3
1

Chart III

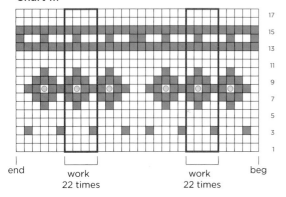

end   work 22 times   work 22 times   beg

17
15
13
11
9
7
5
3
1

BLANKET

With A, CO 99 sts. Do not join. Work 8 rows of St st, ending with a WS row.

Next row (inc): K99, pm, CO 99 sts using backward-loop method—198 sts. Place marker (pm) for beg of rnd and join for working in rnds.

Knit 8 rnds.

Work Chart I, Chart II, Chart III, Chart IV, Chart V, Chart IV, Chart I, Chart II, then Chart III to Row 16.

Next rnd: Work Row 17 over first 99 sts, BO rem 99 sts in patt—99 sts rem.

Work 8 rows of St st. BO all sts.

FINISHING

Work embroidery on front and back foll charts.

Weave in ends.

With RS facing, fold top and bottom edges to back and carefully sew together.

Block to finished measurements.

Chart IV

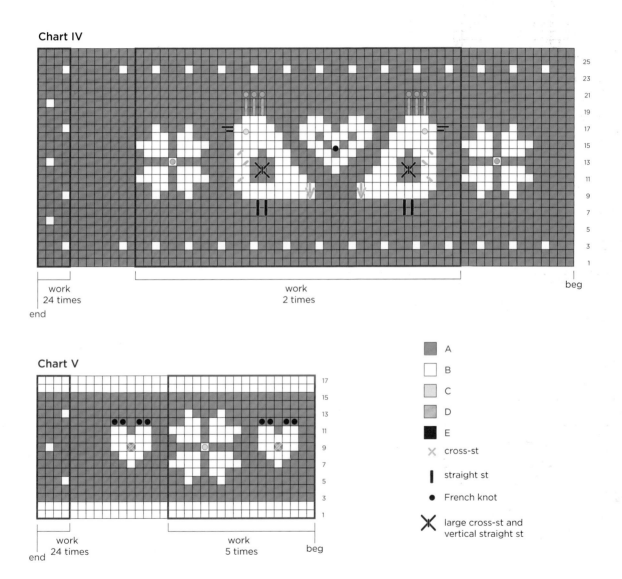

work
24 times

end

work
2 times

beg

Chart V

work
24 times

end

work
5 times

beg

	A
	B
	C
	D
	E
✕	cross-st
I	straight st
●	French knot
✖	large cross-st and vertical straight st

Annelli Doll

ESTONIA

Traditional folk costumes of Estonia are exceptionally varied and beautiful, and they can range from simple gray felted jackets and long coats from Hargla, to elaborately patterned and ribboned headdresses from Kadrina, to astonishingly brightly colored and embroidered knitted festive stockings from Muhu Island. However, it is the traditional summer costume for a young girl from Hargla that was the particular inspiration for this little toy doll. A summer costume would consist of a blue, red, and white striped skirt, an embroidered belt, a simple embroidered blouse, and a garland of summer flowers to decorate her hair.

Annelli is knitted in two flat pieces, with separate arms and legs that are stitched to the body. The details on her blouse, skirt, and boots as well as her eyes, cheeks, and mouth are simple embroidery stitches. Annelli also has little knitted flowers stitched onto her hair. I would recommend using a fine pure wool yarn that will felt slightly once washed, creating a nice firm fabric ideal for toys, and a pure wool fleece toy filler.

FINISHED SIZE
13" (33 cm) tall.

YARN
Sportweight (#2 Fine).

Shown here: Kauni 8/2 wool (100% wool; 574 yd [525 m]/5¼ oz [150 g]): Small amounts of #NN1 natural (A); #PP2 dark brown (B); #QQ3 bright red (C); #SS3 blue (D); #RR dark green (E); #SS1 soft blue (F); #GG deep red (G); #JJ6 soft pink (H).

NEEDLES
Size U.S. 2 (2.75 mm) knitting needles. Adjust needle size if necessary to obtain the correct gauge.

NOTIONS
Tapestry needle, fleece or fiberfill.

GAUGE
26 sts and 34 rows = 4" (10 cm) over St st.

Stitch Guide

Bobble

Work this as tightly as possible for the doll's nose: (K1, turn; p1, turn) twice, sl the st back to right needle, knit into back of the original st, pass first st over the 2nd and off the needle.

DOLL

Front

With C, CO 25 sts.

Work Front chart inc and dec as needed. When working the last few rows at the top of the head, work each section separately, leaving unworked sts on hold. BO rem sts.

Back

Work back same as front through Row 61. Work Back chart Rows 62–92. BO rem sts.

Legs (make 2)

With A, CO 12 sts. Work Leg chart.

Shape Foot

Next row (RS): K9, turn; 3 sts rem unworked.

Next row: P6, turn; 6 sts rem unworked.

Work 12 rows even over center 6 sts still in work.

Next row (RS): Knit to end.

BO all sts pwise.

Arms (make 2)

With D, CO 8 sts. Work Arm chart.

Shape Thumb

Next row (RS): K5, turn; 3 sts rem unworked.

Next row: P2, turn; 6 sts rem unworked.

Work 4 rows even over these 2 sts.

Next row (RS): Knit to end.

Next row: Purl to end; all sts are back in work.

Shape Hand

Next row (dec): K1, ssk, k2, k2tog, k1—2 sts dec'd.

Next row: Purl.

Next row (dec): K1, ssk, k2tog, k1—2 sts dec'd.

Next row (dec): P2tog, ssp—2 sts rem.

Next row (RS): K2tog. Fasten off rem st.

Flowers

With C, CO 5 sts using the cable cast-on method.

*(K1, turn, p1, turn) twice, k1, knit into the base of the first st in the CO edge (there are 2 sts on right needle), pass first st over the 2nd st and off needle; 1 st rem on right needle. Sl next st from left needle to right needle, pass first st over 2nd st and off needle. Sl rem st back to left needle; rep from * 4 more times. Fasten off rem st.

To make a nice flower shape, join the petals into a circle, gathering the CO edge slightly and secure. Thread a contrast yarn up through the center of the flower, *form a loop and secure in the flower CO edge; rep from * 2 more times. Fasten off on WS.

Make 3 more flowers, 1 each in colors D, E, and A.

FINISHING

Embroider the doll foll charts.

Weave in ends.

Handwash all pieces, including the flowers, in warm soapy water and carefully roll up in a towel and gently squeeze out excess water.

Leave to dry flat away from sun or heat source.

Press very lightly with a warm iron over a damp cloth.

Sew arms tog through outside edges of edge sts, leaving ends open. Sew legs tog along outside edges of edge sts. Sew bottom of foot to leg. Stuff arms and legs with fleece or fiberfill.

Sew front and back tog using 1-st seam allowance, leaving CO edges open. Stuff body with fleece or fiberfill; do not sew bottom edge yet.

Sew arms to body at shoulders.

Pin legs to CO edges at bottom of body, leaving about ¼" (0.6 cm) between legs at center. Sew body tog at CO edges and legs.

Using photo as a guide, sew flowers to hair.

Front

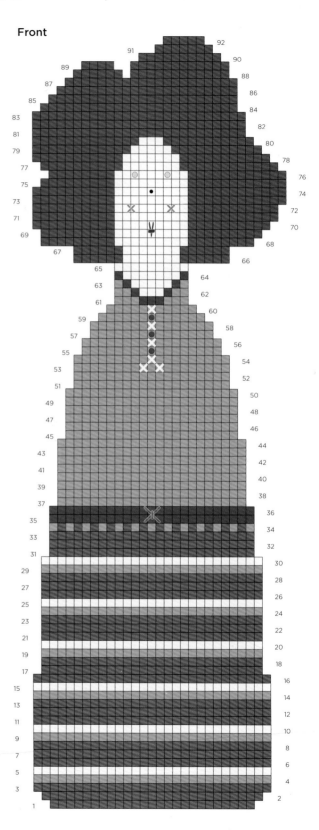

Back

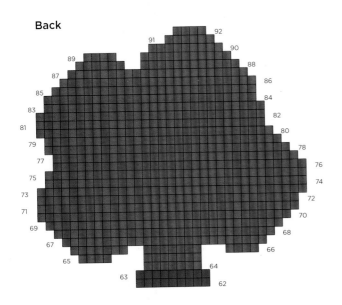

89
91 92
87 90
85 88
83 86
81 84
79 82
77 80
75 78
73 76
71 74
69 72
67 70
65 68
66
64
63 62

Arm

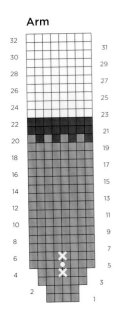

32   31
30   29
28   27
26   25
24   23
22   21
20   19
18   17
16   15
14   13
12   11
10   9
8   7
6   5
4   3
2   1

Leg

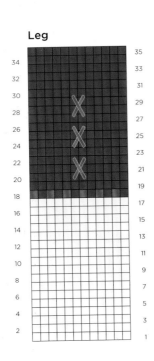

34   35
32   33
30   31
28   29
26   27
24   25
22   23
20   21
18   19
16   17
14   15
12   13
10   11
8   9
6   7
4   5
2   3
            1

Stitch Key

☐ A; k on RS, p on WS

▢• A; bobble

▨ B; k on RS, p on WS

▨ C; k on RS, p on WS

▨ D; k on RS, p on WS

▨ E; k on RS, p on WS

Embroidery Key

▨ F

▨ G

▨ H

✕ cross-st

● French knot

Ѱ straight sts

✕ large cross-st and vertical straight st

Liisi Open Cardigan

ESTONIA

This cardigan was inspired by the tradition of wearing simple and beautifully decorative knitted jackets from the Estonian islands of Saaremaa, Muhu, Kihnu, and Ruhnu, as well as the stunning traditional Estonian knitted lace from Haapsalu. As was common with all northern countries, the cold Baltic climate demanded warm knitwear; knitted items such as stockings, mittens, and jackets were made prolifically by women for both men and women to wear. These jackets often had elaborately embroidered floral panels on the front and around the neck, as well as multicolored decorative crochet borders and cuffs.

Nupps (the pronunciation of which, as Nancy Bush so neatly puts it, "rhymes with soup") are quintessentially Estonian knitted bobbles that are incorporated into many lace patterns. The Liisi Open Cardigan is knitted in a simple lace stitch and has nupps decorating the shoulders as well as small stylized motifs embellished with French knots. A decorative band of several rows of single crochet edge the cardigan, and a tasseled tie is threaded through the front.

FINISHED MEASUREMENTS
29¼ (34½, 39¾, 45, 50¼)" (74.5 [87.5, 101, 114.5, 127.5] cm) bust circumference, to fit bust sizes 32 (37, 43, 48, 52)" (81.5 [94, 109, 122, 134.5] cm). Shown in size 34½" (87.5 cm).

YARN
Sportweight (#2 Fine).

Shown here: Kauni 8/2 Wool (100% wool; 574 yd [525 m]/5¼ oz [150 g]): #NN1 natural (A), 2 (3, 3, 3, 4) balls; #RR7 soft gray blue (B), 1 ball; #QQ bright red (C), small amount needed; #PP2 dark brown (D); small amount needed.

NEEDLES
Size 3 mm (no exact U.S. equivalent; between U.S. sizes 2 and 3) needles: 16" (40 cm) and 32" (80 cm) long circular (cir) and set of 5 double-pointed (dpn). Adjust needle size if necessary to obtain correct gauge.

Size U.S. 1 (2 mm) crochet hook.

NOTIONS
Marker (m), holders, tapestry needle.

GAUGE
27½ sts and 35 rows/rnds = 4" (10 cm) in Vine Lace patt.

Stitch Guide

Estonian 5-stitch Nupps

Row 1 (RS): Working very loosely, work ([k1, yo] 2 times, k1) all in the same stitch—5 nupp stitches are made from 1 stitch.

Row 2: Purl the 5 nupp stitches together—5 nupp stitches decreased back to 1 stitch.

BODY

With longer cir needle and A, CO 201 (237, 273, 309, 345) sts using cable method. Work back and forth, do not join.

Set-up row (WS): P49 (58, 67, 76, 85) for left front, place marker (pm), p103 (121, 139, 157, 175) for back, pm, p49 (58, 67, 76, 85) for right front.

Next row (RS): Work Row 2 of Vine Lace chart as foll: k2, work 9-st rep 5 (6, 7, 8, 9) times, k2, sm, k2, work 9-st rep 11 (13, 15, 17, 19) times, k2, sm, k2, work 9-st rep 5 (6, 7, 8, 9) times, k2.

Work Rows 3 and 4 as established, then rep Rows 1–4 until piece measures about 12 (12½, 12½, 13, 13)" (30.5 [32, 32, 33, 33] cm) from edge, ending with Row 1.

Divide for armholes

Place first 49 (58, 67, 76, 85) sts on holder for right front, place next 103 (121, 139, 157, 175) sts on holder for back—49 (58, 67, 76, 87) sts rem for left front.

LEFT FRONT

Join yarn to beg with Row 2 and work even until armhole measures about 5 (5½, 6, 6½, 7)" (12.5 [14, 15, 16.5, 18] cm), ending with a Row 1.

Nupp Row 1 (RS): K3, *([k1, yo] 2 times, k1) in next st, k3; rep from *, ending k5 (2, 3, 4, 5)—93 (114, 131, 148, 165) sts.

Nupp Row 2: P5 (2, 3, 4, 5), *p5tog, p3; rep from * to end—49 (58, 67, 76, 85) sts rem.

Nupp Row 3: K5, *([k1, yo] 2 times, k1) in next st, k3; rep from * to last 0 (1, 2, 3, 0) st(s), ([k1, yo] 2 times, k1) 0 (0, 0, 1, 0) time, k0 (1, 2, 2, 0)—93 (110, 127, 148, 165) sts.

Nupp Row 4: P3 (4, 5, 2, 3), *p5tog, p3; rep from * to last 10 sts, p5tog, p5—49 (58, 67, 76, 85) sts rem.

Next row (RS): K1, pm, k26 (39, 39, 52, 52), pm, knit rem 22 (18, 27, 23, 32) sts.

Shape Neck

Next row: BO 5 (6, 7, 7, 8) pwise, *purl to m, sl m; rep from * once more, p1—44 (52, 60, 69, 77) sts rem.

Next row: K1, beg Row 1 of color chart for your size and work to m, sm, knit to end.

Work color chart Rows 2–11 between m, BO at beg of WS rows 5 (6, 6, 7, 8) sts once more, then 5 (5, 6, 7, 7) sts—34 (41, 48 55, 62) sts rem. Remove m on last row.

Next row: BO 2, purl to end—32 (39, 46, 53, 60) sts rem.

Next row: Rep Nupp Row 3 to last 3 (2, 1, 0, 3) st(s), ([k1, yo] 2 times, k1) in next st 1 (0, 0, 0, 1) time, k2 (2, 1, 0, 2)—60 (71, 86, 101, 116) sts.

Next row: P2 (5, 4, 3, 2), *p5tog, p3; rep from * to last 2 sts, k2—32 (39, 46, 53, 60) sts rem.

Next row: Rep Nupp Row 1 to last 1 (0, 3, 2, 1) st(s), ([k1, yo] 2 times, k1) in next st 0 (0, 1, 0, 0) time, k1 (0, 2, 2, 1)—60 (75, 90, 101, 116) sts.

Next row: P4 (5, 2, 3, 4), *p5tog, p3; rep from * to end—32 (39, 46, 53, 60) sts rem.

Rep last 4 rows once more.

Knit 1 row even.

Place sts on holder.

RIGHT FRONT

Return 49 (58, 67, 76, 85) held sts for right front to shorter cir needle. Join yarn to beg with Row 2.

Cont even until armhole measures about 5 (5½, 6, 6½, 7)" (12.5 [14, 15, 16.5, 18] cm), ending with a Row 1.

Nupp Row 1 (RS): K5 (2, 3, 4, 5), *([k1, yo] 2 times, k1) in next st, k3; rep from * to end—93 (114, 131, 148, 165) sts.

Nupp Row 2: *P3, p5tog; rep from * to last 5 (2, 3, 4, 5) sts, p5 (2, 3, 4, 5)—49 (58, 67, 76, 85) sts rem.

Nupp Row 3: K3 (4, 5, 2, 3), *([k1, yo] 2 times, k1) in next st, k3; rep from * to last 2 sts, k2—93 (110, 127, 148, 165) sts.

Nupp Row 4: P2, *p3, p5tog; rep from * to last 3 (4, 5, 2, 3) sts, p3 (4, 5, 2, 3)—49 (58, 67, 76, 85) sts rem.

Shape Neck

Next row (RS): BO 5 (6, 7, 7, 8) kwise (1 st rem on right needle), k16 (11, 19, 15, 23) more sts, pm, k26 (39, 39, 52, 52), pm, k1—44 (52, 60, 69, 77) sts rem.

Next row: P1, beg Row 1 of color chart for your size and work to m, sm, knit to end.

Work color chart Rows 2–11 between m, BO at beg of RS rows 5 (6, 6, 7, 8) sts once more, then 5 (5, 6, 7, 7) sts once—34 (41, 48 55, 62) sts rem. Remove m on last row.

Next row: BO 2, knit to end—32 (39, 46, 53, 60) sts rem.

Next row: K2 (5, 4, 3, 2), *([k1, yo] 2 times, k1) in next st, k3; rep from * to last 2 sts, k2—60 (71, 86, 101, 116) sts.

Next row: P2, *p3, p5tog; rep from * to last 2 (5, 4, 3, 2) sts, p2 (5, 4, 3, 2)—32 (39, 46, 53, 60) sts rem.

Next row: K4 (3, 2, 5, 4), *([k1, yo] 2 times, k1) in next st, k3; rep from * to end—60 (75, 90, 101, 116) sts.

Next row: *P3, p5tog; rep from * to last 4 (3, 2, 5, 4) sts, p4 (3, 2, 5, 4)—32 (39, 46, 53, 60) sts rem.

Rep last 4 rows once more.

Knit 2 rows even. Place rem sts on holder.

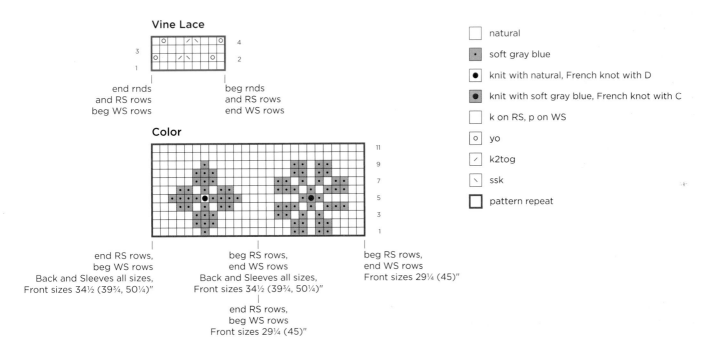

Vine Lace

end rnds
and RS rows
beg WS rows

beg rnds
and RS rows
end WS rows

Color

end RS rows,
beg WS rows
Back and Sleeves all sizes,
Front sizes 34½ (39¾, 50¼)"

beg RS rows,
end WS rows
Back and Sleeves all sizes,
Front sizes 34½ (39¾, 50¼)"

end RS rows,
beg WS rows
Front sizes 29¼ (45)"

beg RS rows,
end WS rows
Front sizes 29¼ (45)"

natural

soft gray blue

knit with natural, French knot with D

knit with soft gray blue, French knot with C

k on RS, p on WS

yo

k2tog

ssk

pattern repeat

BACK

Return 103 (121, 139, 157, 175) held sts for back to longer cir needle. Join yarn to beg with Row 2.

Cont even until armhole measures about 5 (5½, 6, 6½, 7)" (12.5 [14, 15, 16.5, 18] cm), ending with a Row 1.

Nupp Row 1 (RS): K3 (2, 3, 2, 3), *([k1, yo] 2 times, k1) in next st, k3; rep from * to last 4 (3, 4, 3, 4) sts, ([k1, yo] 2 times, k1) in next st, k3 (2, 3, 2, 3)—203 (241, 275, 313, 347) sts.

Nupp Row 2 (WS): P3 (2, 3, 2, 3), *p5tog, p3; rep from * to last 8 (7, 8, 7, 8) sts, p5tog, p3 (2, 3, 2, 3)—103 (121, 139, 157, 175) sts.

Nupp Row 3: K5 (4, 5, 4, 5), *([k1, yo] 2 times, k1) in next st, k3; rep from * to last 6 (5, 6, 5, 6) sts, ([k1, yo] 2 times, k1) in next st, k5 (4, 5, 4, 5)—199 (237, 271, 309, 343) sts.

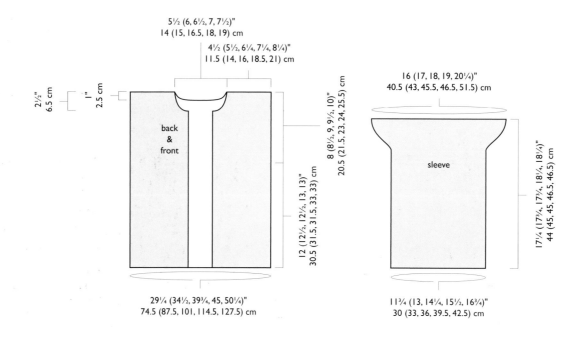

Nupp Row 4: P5 (4, 5, 4, 5), *p5tog, p3; rep from * to last 2 (1, 2, 1, 2) st(s), p2 (1, 2, 1, 2)—103 (121, 139, 157, 175) sts rem.

Work 2 rows even in St st.

Next row (RS): K6 (2, 11, 7, 3), beg Row 1 of color chart as indicated and work last 13 sts of rep 1 time, work 26-st rep 3 (4, 4, 5, 6) times, k6 (2, 11, 7, 3).

Next row: P6 (2, 11, 7, 3), work 26-st rep 3 (4, 4, 5, 6) times, then work 13 sts, p6 (2, 11, 7, 3).

Cont color chart as established.

Work 1 WS row.

Right Shoulder

Nupp Row 1 (RS): K5 (4, 5, 4, 5), *([k1, yo] 2 times, k1) in next st, k3; rep from * 7 (9, 10, 13, 16) more times, ([k1, yo] 2 times, k1) in next st, k2 (4, 4, 4, 2), place rem 69 (80, 91, 102, 113) sts on holder—70 (85, 96, 115, 134) sts.

Nupp Row 2: P2 (4, 4, 4, 2), *p5tog, p3; rep from * to last 5 (4, 5, 4, 5) sts, p5 (4, 5, 4, 5)—34 (41, 48, 55, 62) sts rem.

Nupp Row 3 (RS): K3 (2, 3, 2, 3), *([k1, yo] 2 times, k1) in next st, k3; rep from * 7 (9, 10, 13, 16) more times, ([k1, yo] 2 times, k1) in next st, k3 (5, 5, 5, 3)—70 (85, 96, 115, 134) sts.

Nupp Row 4: BO 1 st, 1 st rem on right needle, p1 (3, 3, 3, 1), *p5tog, p3; rep from * to last 3 (2, 3, 2, 3) sts, p3 (2, 3, 2, 3)—33 (40, 47, 54, 61) sts rem.

Nupp Row 5 (RS): K5 (4, 5, 4, 5), *([k1, yo] 2 times, k1) in next st, k3; rep from * 6 (9, 10, 13, 15) more times, ([k1, yo] 2 times, k1) in next st, k5 (3, 3, 3, 5)—65 (84, 95, 114, 129) sts.

Nupp Row 6: P5 (3, 3, 3, 5), *p5tog, p3; rep from * to last 5 (4, 5, 4, 5) sts, p5 (4, 5, 4, 5)—33 (40, 47, 54, 61) sts rem.

Nupp Row 7: Rep Nupp Row 3—70 (85, 96, 115, 134) sts.

Nupp Row 8: BO 1 st, 1 st rem on right needle, p1 (3, 3, 3, 1), *p5tog, p3; rep from * to last 3 (2, 3, 2, 3) sts, p3 (2, 3, 2, 3)—32 (39, 46, 53, 60) sts rem.

Knit 1 row even. Place rem sts on holder.

Shape Neck

Return held 69 (80, 91, 102, 113) sts to shorter cir needle. Join yarn to beg with a RS row.

Left Shoulder

Nupp Row 1 (RS): BO 35 (39, 43, 47, 51) for neck, 1 st rem on right needle, k1 (3, 3, 3, 1), *([k1, yo] 2 times, k1) in next st, k3; rep from * 7 (9, 10, 13, 16) more times, ([k1, yo] 2 times, k1) in next st, k5 (4, 5, 4, 5)—70 (85, 96, 115, 134) sts rem.

Nupp Row 2: P5 (4, 5, 4, 6), *p5tog, p3; rep from * to last 2 (4, 4, 4, 2) sts, p2 (4, 4, 4, 2)—34 (41, 48, 55, 62) sts rem.

Nupp Row 3 (RS): BO 1 st, 1 st rem on right needle, k2 (4, 4, 4, 2), *([k1, yo] 2 times, k1) in next st, k3; rep from * 7 (9, 10, 13, 16) more times, ([k1, yo] 2 times, k1) in next st, k3 (2, 3, 2, 3)—69 (84, 95, 114, 133) sts.

Work Rows 2–4 as established, then rep Rows 1–4 until piece measures about 13¾ (14¼, 14¼, 14¾, 14¾)" (35 [36, 36, 37.5, 37.5] cm) from edge, ending with Row 4.

Next rnd: Knit and inc 1 (0, 1, 0 1) st—86 (94, 104, 112, 122) sts.

Top of Sleeve
Beg working back and forth.

Nupp Row 1 (RS): K3 (3, 4, 4, 3), pm, *([k1, yo] 2 times, k1) in next st, k3; rep from * to last 3 (3, 4, 4, 3) sts, ([k1, yo] 2 times, k1) in next st, pm, k2 (2, 3, 3, 2)—170 (186, 204, 220, 242) sts.

Nupp Row 2 (WS): P2 (2, 3, 3, 2), sm, *p5tog, p3; rep from * to last 0 (0, 1, 1, 0) st and sm when you come to it, p0 (0, 1, 1, 0)—86 (94, 104, 112, 122) sts rem.

Nupp Row 3 (inc): K1, M1, knit to m, sm, k2, *([k1, yo] 2 times, k1) in next st, k3; rep from * to 2 sts before m, ([k1, yo] 2 times, k1) in next st, k1, sm, knit to last st, M1, k1— 172 (188, 206, 222, 244) sts.

Nupp Row 4: Purl to m, sm, p1, *p5tog, p3; rep from * to 7 sts before m, p5tog, p2, sm, purl to end—88 (96, 106, 114, 124) sts rem.

Row 5 (inc): K1, M1, knit and remove m, M1, k1—2 sts inc'd.

Row 6 (inc): P1, M1P, purl to last st, M1P, p1—2 sts inc'd.

Row 7 (inc): K1, M1, k 0 (4, 9, 0, 5), pm, beg Row 1 of color chart for sleeve and work last 13 sts of rep, then work 26-st rep 3 (3, 3, 4, 4) times, then knit to end and at the same time, when 1 st rem, M1, knit last st—2 sts inc'd.

Rep inc row every row 11 (11, 9, 9, 8) more times—116 (124, 130, 138, 146) sts. Work even if necessary until chart is complete. Work 3 more rows even.

Nupp Row 1 (RS): K3 (3, 4, 4, 4), *([k1, yo] 2 times, k1) in next st, k3; rep from * to last 1 (1, 2, 2, 2) st(s), knit to end—228 (244, 254, 270, 286) sts.

Nupp Row 2: P2 (2, 3, 3, 3), *p5tog, p3; rep from * to last 8 (8, 9, 9, 9) sts, p5tog, p3 (3, 4, 4, 4)—116 (124, 130, 138, 146) sts.

Nupp Row 3: K5 (5, 2, 2, 2), *([k1, yo] 2 times, k1) in next st, k3; rep from * to last 3 (3, 4, 4, 4) sts, ([k1, yo] 2 times, k1) in next st, k2 (2, 3, 3, 3)—228 (244, 258, 274, 290) sts.

Nupp Row 4: P3 (2, 3, 2, 3), *p5tog, p3; rep from * to last 3 (5, 5, 5, 3) sts, p3 (5, 5, 5, 3)—33 (40, 47, 54, 61) sts rem.

Nupp Row 5 (RS): K5 (3, 3, 3, 5), *([k1, yo] 2 times, k1) in next st, k3; rep from * 6 (9, 10, 13, 15) more times, ([k1, yo] 2 times, k1) in next st, k5 (4, 5, 4, 5)—65 (84, 95, 114, 129) sts.

Nupp Row 6: P5 (4, 5, 4, 5), *p5tog, p3; rep from * to last 5 (3, 3, 3, 5) sts, p5 (3, 3, 3, 5)—33 (40, 47, 54, 61) sts rem.

Nupp Row 7: BO 1 st, 1 st rem on right needle, k1 (3, 3, 3, 1), *([k1, yo] 2 times, k1) in next st, k3; rep from * 7 (9, 10, 13, 16) more times, ([k1, yo] 2 times, k1) in next st, k3 (2, 3, 2, 3)—68 (83, 94, 113, 132) sts.

Nupp Row 8: P3 (2, 3, 2, 3), *p5tog, p3; rep from * to last 2 (4, 4, 4, 2) sts, p2 (4, 4, 4, 2)—32 (39, 46, 53, 60) sts rem.

Return sts for left front on dpn. Hold needles with WS tog and join shoulder using three-needle BO on RS. Rep with right shoulder.

SLEEVES (MAKE 2)
With dpn and A, CO 85 (94, 103, 112, 121) sts using the cable method. Pm for beg of rnd and join for working in rnds.

Rnd 1: Work Row 1 of Vine Lace chart as foll: k2, work 9-st rep 9 (10, 11, 12, 13) times, k2.

Nupp Row 4: P2 (2, 3, 3, 3), *p5tog, p3; rep from * to last 10 (10, 7, 7, 7) sts, p5tog, p5 (5, 2, 2, 2)—116 (124, 130, 138, 146) sts.

Rep Nupp Rows 1–4 once more.

Knit 2 rows even.

With shorter cir needle and A, with RS facing, beg at bottom of armhole and pick up and knit 116 (124, 130, 138, 146) sts evenly around armhole.

Pm for beg of rnd and join for working in rnds.

Knit 1 rnd.

Turn body with WS facing. Hold body and sleeve with WS tog with open edge of sleeve at bottom of armhole. Join pieces using three-needle BO on RS.

CROCHET EDGING

With crochet hook and D, with RS facing, join yarn to bottom edge at center of back with a sl st, work sc in every st along CO edge, hold right front with first 2 sts folded to WS, work 3 sc in corner st, 1 sc in every other row to neck edge, 3 sc in corner, 1 sc in every other st and row along neck edge to 2 sts before left corner, hold left front with first 2 sts folded to WS, work 3 sc in corner, 1 sc in every other row along front edge, 3 sc in bottom corner, 1 sc in every st along CO edge. With C, sl st in ch-1 at beg of rnd to join.

Rnd 2: Ch 1, work sc in each sc around, working 2 sc in each corner. With B, sl st in ch-1 at beg of rnd.

Rnd 3: Ch 1, work sc in each sc around, sl st in ch-1 at beg of rnd. Fasten off.

Rep crochet edging along CO edges of sleeves, working sc in each st around.

FINISHING

Embroider French knots foll Color chart.

Sew sleeve seams.

Weave in ends.

I-Cord (make 2)

With 2 dpn and A, CO 2 sts.

Work I-cord until piece measures about 19" (48.5 cm). BO.

With A, make 2 tassels about 1¾" (4.5 cm) long.

Attach tassel to one end of cord. Thread rem end of cord through front below end of lace using photo as guide. Sew cord to armhole seam.

Handwash in warm soapy water and carefully roll up in a towel and gently squeeze out excess water.

Reshape and leave to dry flat away from sun or heat source.

Press very lightly with a warm iron over a damp cloth.

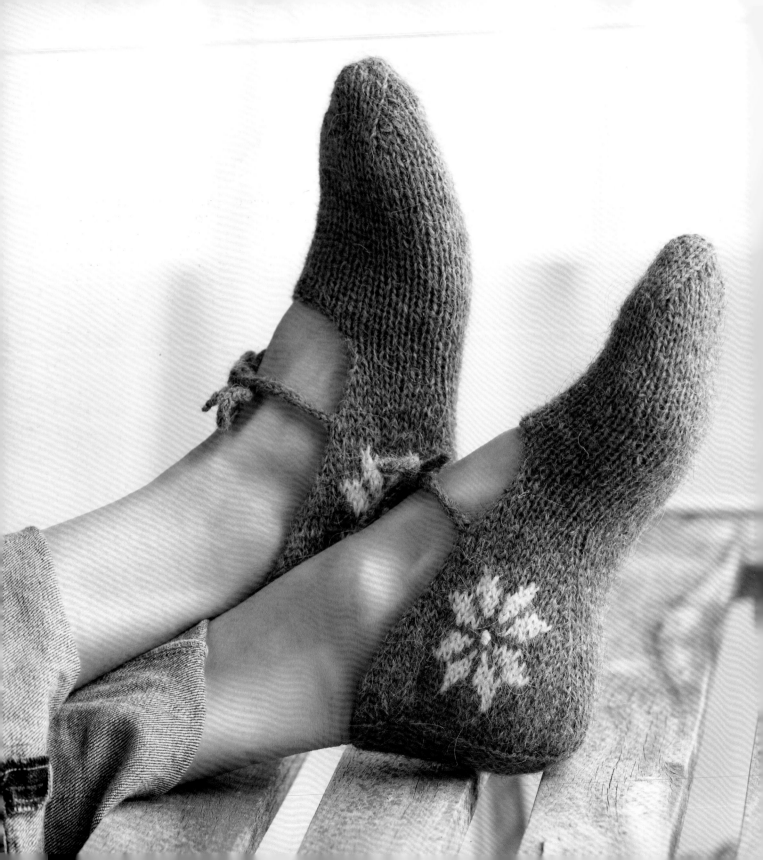

Noomi Slippers

FAROE ISLANDS

Traditionally, in Scandinavian homes, shoes are left at the door; only slippers, which are invariably made from wool, are worn inside. On the Faroe Islands, *skóleistur*—knitted short slipper-like wool socks that were usually patterned and double thick—were always worn around the house. Skóleistur could also be worn as an extra layer of insulation against the elements, lining outdoor boots. They could even be pulled on over the top of the boots or other shoes to prevent slipping on wet ground or ice and snow.

The Noomi slippers are inspired by these traditional Faroese skóleistur. They are knitted in the round on double-pointed needles with a warm, comfortable lining, making them twice as thick and extra durable. The slippers are adorned with a traditional Nordic eight-point star with a single French knot in its center. The star is a classic motif that is now closely associated with Scandinavian knitwear and is a derivation of ancient sun and moon circular motifs and patterns. These patterns were associated with the powerful forces of the cosmos and were believed to offer the wearer protection from evil spirits. An I-cord is used to make simple ties, helping to keep the slippers on. These slippers are also fulled slightly before wearing.

FINISHED MEASUREMENTS

9″ (23 cm) long from heel.

YARN

Fingering weight (#1 Super Fine).

Shown here: Sirri 2-Ply (100% wool; 273 yd [250 m]/100 g): #31 natural light brown (A), 1 skein; #10 natural ecru (B), 1 skein (only a small amount is needed).

NEEDLES

Set of 5 size 3 mm (no exact U.S. equivalent; between U.S. sizes 2 and 3) double-pointed needles (dpn). Adjust needle size as necessary to obtain the correct gauge.

NOTIONS

Marker (m), tapestry needle.

GAUGE

23 sts and 32 rows = 4″ (10 cm) in stockinette stitch.

OUTER SLIPPER (MAKE 2)

Heel

*With A, CO 12 sts. Work back and forth in St st for 34 rows. Cut the yarn.

With RS facing, pick up and knit 33 sts along right edge of heel, knit 12 heel sts, then pick up and knit 33 sts along left edge of heel—78 sts.

Arrange the sts over 3 dpn, with 33 sts on Needle 1, 12 sts on Needle 2, and 33 sts on Needle 3. Do not join.

Instep

Work 3 rows of St st, ending with a WS row. At the same time, work chart over sts on Needles 1 and 3 using intarsia technique.

Next (dec) row (RS): K1, ssk, knit to last 3 sts on Needle 1, ssk, k1; k12 on Needle 2; k1, k2tog, knit to last 3 sts on Needle 3, k2tog, k1—4 sts dec'd.

Next row (WS) Purl.

Rep last 2 rows 11 more times—30 sts rem; 9 sts each on Needles 1 and 3 and 12 sts on Needle 2.

Foot

Next row (RS): Knit to end of row, CO 6 sts using backward-loop method—36 sts.

Divide sts evenly over 4 dpn (9 sts on each needle). Place marker (pm) for beg of rnd and join for working in rnds.*

Work 30 rnds of St st.

Note: Try on slipper as you work and add or decrease the number of rounds worked for the correct length from the heel.

Shape Toe

Rnd 1: *Knit to last 2 sts of needle, k2tog; rep from * three more times—4 sts dec'd.

Rnd 2: Knit.

Rep Rnds 1 and 2 six more times—8 sts rem.

Cut the yarn, leaving an 8" (20.5 cm) tail, thread through rem sts, pull tight to close hole, fasten off on WS.

INNER LINING (MAKE 2)

Make inner lining same as outer slipper from * to *, omitting chart.

Work 27 rnds of St st, or 3 fewer rnds than outer slipper if length was changed.

Shape toe same as outer slipper.

FINISHING

Embroider French knots foll chart.

Weave in all ends.

Place inner lining inside outer slipper with WS tog, sew tog along CO sts at front of opening, using backstitch. Do not join rem of opening at this time.

Sew a couple of sts to join toe of inner lining to outer slipper on WS.

Turn piece with outer slipper on RS and inner lining on inside, and with WS tog, sew rem opening using overcast st along edges, sewing firmly but not too tightly (the opening must remain stretchy).

I-Cord Ties

With 1 dpn and A, pick up and k3 sts along one edge foll chart. Work I-cord for 10 rows.

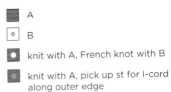

Next (dec) row: K1, k2tog—2 sts rem.

Cont I-cord over rem sts until tie measures 7" (18 cm).

Next row: Skp—1 st rem. Cut yarn and fasten off by knotting yarn several times before threading it down through the cord.

Wash slippers in warm soapy water.

Pat dry with a towel. Reshape and leave to dry flat out of direct sunlight.

When dry, press lightly with a warm iron over damp cloth.

Oluffa Doorstop

FAROE ISLANDS

Oluffa will make a wonderful gift at any time of the year, but perhaps especially so in the early months as we look forward to the lengthening, lighter days. Chickens and cockerels were considered to be symbols of protection and good luck; in folklore, they were particularly associated with the sunrise, daylight, and spring. Consequently, they were considered potent protection against the dangers that came with darkness and winter.

Oluffa is knitted in the round using a selection of traditional Faroese patterns and Nordic eight-point stars that are highlighted with simple French knots. I would recommend filling it with natural sheep's fleece and a strategically placed rock or other weighty object in the base.

FINISHED MEASUREMENTS
10½" (26.5 cm) wide and 10½" (26.5 cm) high.

YARN
Fingering weight (#1 Super Fine).

Shown here: Sirri 2-Ply (100% wool; 273 yd [250 m]/100 g): natural ecru (A), 1 skein; #C7 blue (B), 1 skein; #C4 orange (C), 1 skein (only a small amount needed).

NEEDLES
Size 3 mm (no exact U.S. equivalent; between U.S. sizes 2 and 3) needles: 24" (60 cm) long circular (cir) needle and set of 5 double-pointed (dpn).

NOTIONS
Markers (m), holders or waste yarn, tapestry needle, fleece or fiberfill, small beanbags or rock (optional).

GAUGE
26 sts and 26 rnds = 4" (10 cm) over chart patt.

Stitch Guide

Left Slant Increase (M1L): With left needle tip, lift the strand between the needles from the front to back, then knit the lifted loop through the back.

Right Slant Increase (M1R): With left needle tip, lift the strand between the needles from back to front, then knit the lifted loop through the front.

☐	A
⊡	B
⊙	k with B, bullion st with C
●	k with A, bullion st with C
☒	k with B, cross-st with C
∨	k with A, duplicate st with B

NOTES

Use Left Slant Increase 1 stitch after marker and Right Slant Increase 1 stitch before marker, keeping 2 knit stitches between increases.

Use ssk to decrease 1 stitch after marker and k2tog to decrease 1 stitch before marker, keeping 2 knit stitches between decreases.

BODY

With cir needle or dpn and A, CO 132 sts. Place marker (pm) for beg of rnd and join for working in rnds. Place 2nd m after 66 sts. If using dpn, divide sts evenly over 4 needles (33 sts on each needle).

Work chart as foll: beg at right edge of chart and work to left edge of chart, sm, beg at left edge of chart and work to right edge of chart. Cont chart as established through Rnd 36—150 sts.

Head

Change to dpn if using cir needle.

Rnd 37: Work 25 sts, place next 100 sts on holder or waste yarn for back and tail, pm, work rem 25 sts —50 sts.

Work Rnds 38–65 of chart—16 sts rem.

Place rem sts on holders or waste yarn.

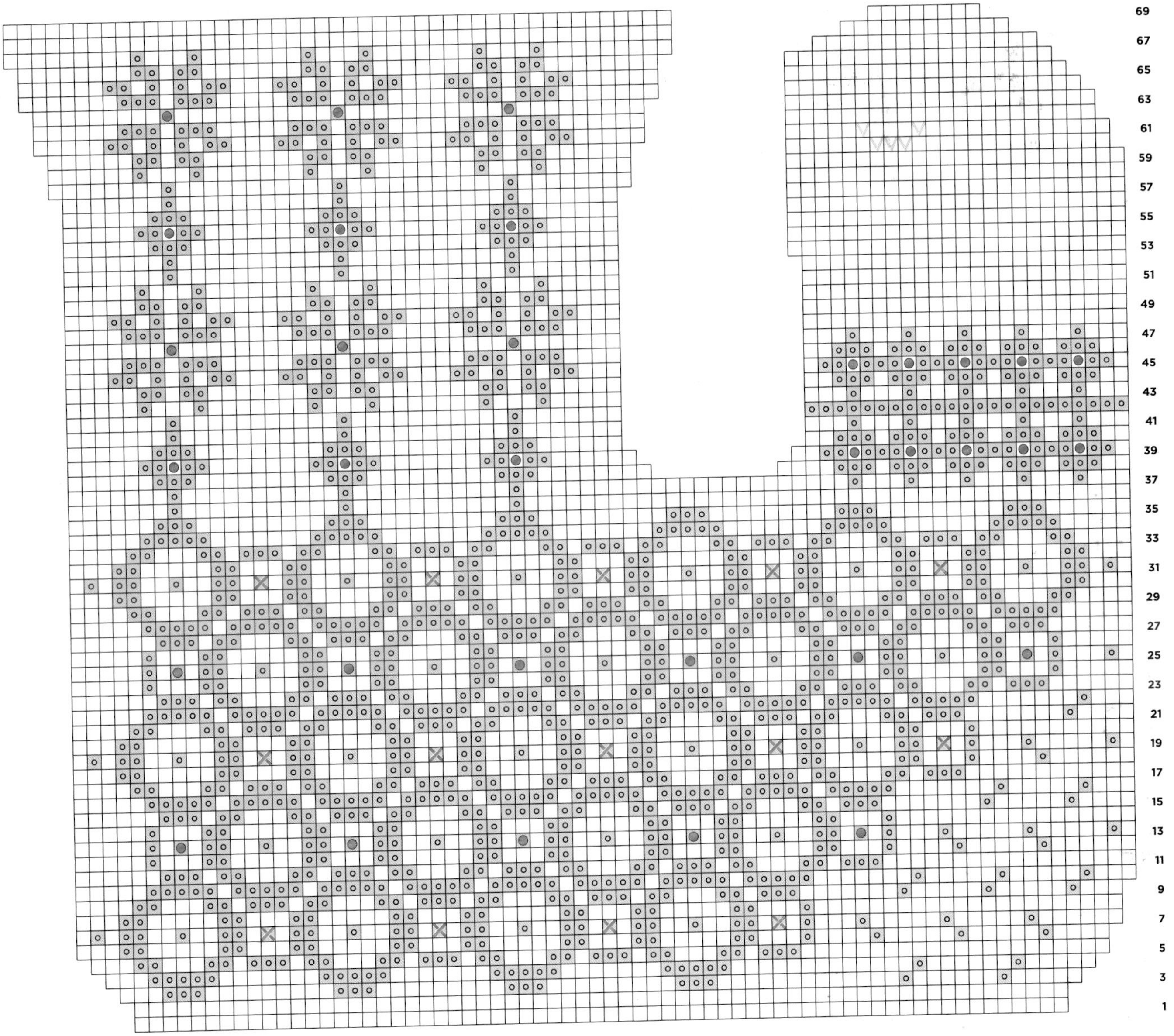
69
67
65
63
61
59
57
55
53
51
49
47
45
43
41
39
37
35
33
31
29
27
25
23
21
19
17
15
13
11
9
7
5
3
1

Tail

Rnd 37: Place first 9 sts on holder or waste yarn for back, using dpn, work 41 sts foll chart, pm, work next 41 sts foll chart as established, place rem 9 sts on holder or waste yarn for back—82 sts on needles. Pm for beg of rnd and join for working in rnds.

Work Rnds 38–65 of chart—94 sts rem.

Place rem sts on holders or waste yarn.

Beak

With dpn and C, CO 22 sts. Divide sts over 4 needles with 5 sts each on Needles 1 and 3 and 6 sts each on Needles 2 and 4. Pm for beg of rnd and join for working in the rnd.

Rnd 1: Knit.

Rnd 2 (dec): K1, ssk, knit to last 3 sts, k2tog, k1—2 sts dec'd.

Rep Rnd 2 eight more times—4 sts rem.

Next rnd (dec): (K2tog) twice, pass first st over 2nd and off needle. Fasten off rem st.

Comb (make 3)

With dpn and B, CO 20 sts. Divide sts evenly over 4 needles (5 sts on each needle). Pm for beg of rnd and join for working in rnds.

Rnds 1–4: Knit.

Rnd 5 (dec): K1, ssk, knit to last 3 sts on second needle, k2tog, k2, ssk, knit to last 3 sts on fourth needle, k2tog, k1—4 sts dec'd.

Rnd 6: Knit.

Rnds 7 and 8: Rep Rnd 5—8 sts rem.

Cut yarn, leaving an 8″ (20.5 cm) tail, thread through rem sts, pull tight to close hole, fasten off on WS.

Bottom

With dpn and A, CO 3 sts. Do not join but work back and forth using 2 needles.

Row 1: Knit.

Row 2: Purl.

Row 3: K1, M1L, knit to last st, M1R, k1—2 sts inc'd.

Rep Rows 2 and 3 five more times—15 sts.

Work even in St st until piece measures 9½" (24 cm) from beg, ending with a WS row.

Next row (dec): K1, ssk, knit to last 3 sts, k2tog, k1—2 sts dec'd.

Next row: Purl.

Rep last 2 rows 4 more times—5 sts rem.

Next row (RS): K1, k3tog, k1—3 sts rem.

Next row: Purl.

Next row: K3tog—1 st rem. Fasten off rem st.

FINISHING

With C, embroider both sides of body using bullion st, cross-st and duplicate st foll chart.

Turn piece with WS facing, return sts from holders or waste yarn at head to dpn. Join sts using three-needle BO. Rep with rem sts for back and tail.

Weave in ends.

Wash all the pieces in warm soapy water.

Pat dry with a towel. Reshape and leave to dry flat and out of sun or direct heat.

When dry, press lightly with a warm iron over a damp cloth.

Fill head and tail with fleece or fiberfill.

Sew bottom to CO edge of body using backstitch, leaving about 3" (7.5 cm) to 4" (10 cm) open at tail end.

Cont filling body until nice and firm but not too full so as to distort the pattern. If desired, slip small beanbags into bottom. Finish sewing bottom to CO edge of body.

Evenly fill the beak and 3 comb pieces. Sew CO edges of each piece, leaving a 10" (25.5 cm) tail.

Using the photo as a guide, carefully sew beak and comb pieces to the bird's head.

Marna Woman's Cape

FAROE ISLANDS

Large practical shawls were traditionally made in all of the northern countries and would have been worn both indoors and out. They were commonly knitted in triangular shapes, which could be tied securely across the chest, around the back, and then brought to the front again and tied at the waist. This ensured that they stayed in place when women were working in the home or outdoors in the fields. Often these shawls would have been knitted in garter stitch (so that both sides would be the same) and in naturally occurring tones of yarn.

The traditional shawls knitted on the Faroe Islands differ from those knitted in other northern countries, as they have an extra panel (or gore) in the center that narrows toward the top, as well as extra concealed shaping at the shoulders—both of which contribute to creating a distinctively more secure and snug fit. The Marna cape is a simplified adaptation of the traditional Faroese shawl, as you will not be able to tie it at the back, but it does have shoulder shaping.

FINISHED MEASUREMENTS
66" (167.5 cm) bottom circumference.

YARN
Fingering weight (#1 Super Fine).

Shown here: Sirri 2-ply (100% wool; 273 yd [250 m]/100 g): #10 natural ecru (A), 2 skeins; #20 natural light gray (B), 2 skeins.

NEEDLES
Size 3 mm (no exact U.S. equivalent; between U.S. sizes 2 and 3) needles: 32" (80 cm) long circular (cir) and 2 double-pointed (dpn). Adjust needle size if necessary to obtain the correct gauge.

NOTIONS
Markers (m), tapestry needle, two 1¼" (32 mm) buttons.

GAUGE
23 sts and 38 rows = 4" (10 cm) in garter stitch worked in rows.

Stitch Guide

Stripe Pattern

(any number of sts)

*2 rows with B, 2 rows with A.

Rep from * for Stripe patt.

Picot Edging

(using a cable cast-on)

1. Make a loop stitch and place on double-pointed needle.

2. Knit into the loop stitch and leave stitch just made on the right needle, bring the left needle tip around and through the front of the stitch to slip it onto the left needle to twist it.

3. *Insert right needle tip between the first and second stitches on the left needle and place the stitch just formed on the left needle tip in the same way as the first knit stitch. Repeat from * once more—4 stitches on left needle.

4. Bind off 3 stitches—1 stitch remains, and 1 picot made.

5. Slip the remaining stitch to the opposite end of the needle.

Repeat Steps 2-5, beginning each repeat by knitting into the stitch remaining on the left needle.

NOTES

Change colors at the end of rows by dropping the old color and picking up the new color from under the old color.

Markers are used to indicate where to work decreases; slip markers as you come to them.

CAPE

With dpn and A, make 195 picots. Fasten off rem st but do not cut yarn.

Change to cir needle and B. Pick up and knit 2 sts in each picot across—390 sts.

Row 1 (WS): Knit.

Row 2 (dec): Drop B and pick up A. K5, *ssk, k166, k2tog*, k40; rep from * to * once more, k5—386 sts.

Row 3: K5, *k1, yo; rep from * to last 6 sts, k6—761 sts.

Row 4: Drop A and pick up B. Knit.

Row 5: K5, *k2tog, rep from * to last 6 sts, k6—386 sts.

Rows 6 and 7: Change to A. K6, *yo, k2tog; rep from * to last 6 sts, k6.

Row 8: Change to B. K5, place marker (pm), k169, pm, k38, pm, k169, pm, k5.

Row 9 (dec): K5, ssk, knit to 3 sts before next m, k2tog, k19, k2tog, k19, ssk, knit to 2 sts before last m, k2tog, k1, k5—381 sts. Cut B.

Rows 10-13: With A, knit.

Row 14 (dec): K5, ssk, knit to 3 sts before next m, k2tog, knit to next m, k1, ssk, knit to 2 sts before last m, k2tog, k5—377 sts.

Row 15: K22, *ssk, yo, k1, yo, k2tog, k3*; rep from * to * to 12 sts before next m, k20, rep from * to * to 5 sts before next m, rep from * to * to 5 sts before next m, k20, rep from * to * to last 19 sts, knit to end.

Row 16: Knit.

Row 17: K23, *yo, s2kp2, yo, k5*; rep from * to * to 11 sts before next m, k20, rep from * to * 4 sts before next m, k20, rep from * to * last 18 sts, knit to end.

Row 18 (dec): Rep Row 14—373 sts.

Row 19: K21, *ssk, yo, k1, yo, k2tog, k3*; rep from * to * to 11 sts before next m, k19, rep from * to * to 5 sts before next m, k19, rep from * to * to last 18 sts, knit to end.

Rows 20–21: Knit.

Row 22 (dec): Rep Row 14—369 sts.

Rows 23–24: Knit.

Row 25: K16, *ssk, yo, k1, yo, k2tog, k3*; rep from * to * to 6 sts before next m, k10, rep from * to * to 1 st before next m, k10, rep from * to * to last 13 sts, knit to end.

Row 26 (dec): Rep Row 12—365 sts.

Row 27: K16, *yo, s2kp2, yo, k5*; rep from * to * to 4 sts before next m, k9, rep from * to * to next m, k9, rep from * to * to last 11 sts, knit to end.

Row 28: Knit.

Row 29: K15, *ssk, yo, k1, yo, k2tog, k3; rep from * to * to 5 sts before next m, k9, rep from * to * to 1 st before next m, k9, rep from * to * to last 12 sts, knit to end.

Row 30 (dec): Rep Row 14—361 sts.

Rows 31–33: Knit.

Row 34 (dec): Rep Row 14—357 sts.

Row 35: K17, *ssk, yo, k1, yo, k2tog, k3; rep from * to * to 7 sts before next m, k15, rep from * to * to 5 sts before next m, k15, rep from * to * to last 14 sts, knit to end.

Row 36: Knit.

Row 37: K18, *yo, s2kp2, yo, k5*; rep from * to * to 5 sts before next m, k14, rep from * to * to 4 sts before next m, k15, rep from * to * to last 13 sts, knit to end.

Row 38 (dec): Rep Row 14—353 sts.

Row 39: K16, *ssk, yo, k1, yo, k2tog, k3; rep from * to * to 6 sts before next m, k14, rep from * to * to 5 sts before next m, k14, rep from * to * to last 13 sts, knit to end.

Rows 40–41: Knit.

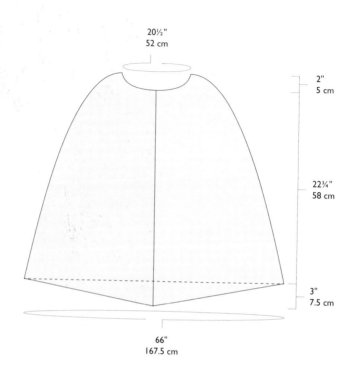

20½"
52 cm

2"
5 cm

22¾"
58 cm

3"
7.5 cm

66"
167.5 cm

Row 42 (dec): Rep Row 14—349 sts.

Row 43: Knit.

Beg Stripe patt, working as foll:

Rows 44–45: Knit.

Row 46 (dec): K5, ssk, knit to 3 sts before next m, k2tog, knit to next m, k1, ssk, knit to 2 sts before last m, k2tog, k5—4 sts dec'd.

Row 47: Knit.

Rows 38–83: Rep Rows 44–47 nine more times—309 sts.

Rows 84–85: Knit.

Row 86 (dec): K5, ssk, knit to 3 sts before next m, k2tog, k5,

ssk, knit to 6 sts before next m, k2tog, k5, ssk, knit to 2 sts before next m, k2tog, k5—303 sts.

Row 87: Knit.

Rows 88–123: Rep Rows 44–47 nine times—267 sts.

Rows 124–204: Rep Rows 84–123 twice—183 sts.

Rows 205–206: Knit.

Row 207 (dec): (K5, ssk) 5 times, (k5, k2tog) 5 times, k3, k2tog, k1, (ssk, k5) twice, ssk, (k5, k2tog) twice, k1, ssk, k3, (ssk, k5) 5 times, (k2tog, k5) 5 times—156 sts.

Rows 208–209: Knit and remove m.

Cut B and cont garter st with A.

Shape shoulders

Row 210 (dec): K42, pm, ssk, k10, k2tog, pm, k44 sts, pm, k2tog, k10, ssk, pm, knit rem 42 sts—152 sts.

Row 211: Knit.

Row 212 (dec): *Knit to m, ssk, knit to 2 sts before next m, k2tog; rep from * once more, knit to end—4 sts dec'd.

Rows 213–220: Rep Rows 211 and 212 four more times—132 sts rem.

Row 221: Knit.

BO as foll: k42, ssk, k16, ssk, k8, ssk, k16, ssk, k42.

I-Cord Button Loop

With dpn and A, CO 2 sts.

Work I-cord until piece measures about 4" (10 cm) long.

BO.

Sew loop to WS of right front below neck using photo as guide to placement.

FINISHING

Weave in all ends.

Wash the cape in warm soapy water. Pat dry with a towel and leave to dry flat out of direct sunlight.

When dry, press lightly with a warm iron over damp cloth.

Sew buttons to front edges at neck.

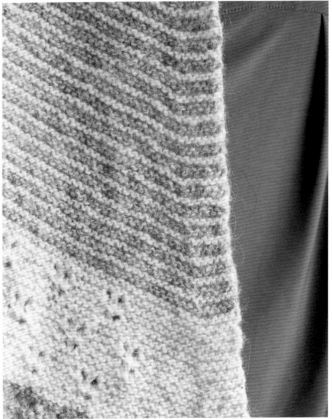

Onni Child's Sweater and Hat

FINLAND

The National Museum of Finland in Helsinki (www.nba.fi) has many examples of white linen shifts and samplers embroidered with traditional red hooked motifs. These stylized motifs are simplified, abstract forms of horned animals, which have their origins in shamanism. These animals were once considered to have significant magical powers and were believed to be able to confuse the evil eye, especially if placed strategically around the hems and cuffs of garments. The Onni hat and sweater have been inspired by these abstract designs and also by the traditional seed-stitch patterning that was commonly used in Finland on knitted sweaters and other knitted items toward the end of the nineteenth century.

SWEATER

FINISHED MEASUREMENTS

27 (29, 31, 33, 35)" (68.5 [73.5, 78.5, 84, 89] cm) chest circumference. Sweater shown measures 29" (73.5 cm).

YARN

Fingering weight (#1 Super Fine).

Shown here: Riihivila Aarni (100% wool; 131 yd [120 m]/3½ oz [100 g]): #1006 natural beige (A), 2 (2, 2, 3, 3) balls; #3330 soft blue (B), 1 (1, 1, 1, 2) ball(s); #3394 soft red (C), 1 (1, 1, 2, 2) ball(s); #3283 light orange (D), 1 ball; #3306 soft yellow (E), 1 ball.

NEEDLES

Size 3 (no exact U.S. equivalent; between U.S. sizes 2 and 3) needles: 24" (60 cm) circular (cir), and set of 5 double-pointed (dpn). Adjust needle size if necessary to obtain the correct gauge.

NOTIONS

Markers (m), holder, tapestry needle.

GAUGE

24½ sts and 30 rows = 4" (10 cm) in main patt chart work in rounds.

HAT

FINISHED MEASUREMENTS

20" (51 cm) circumference.

YARN

Fingering weight (#1 Super Fine).

Shown here: Riihivila Aarni (100% wool; 131 yd [120 m]/3½ oz [100 g]): #1006 natural beige (A), 2 skeins; #3330 soft blue (B), 1 skein; #3394 soft red (C), 1 skein; #3283 light orange (D), 1 skein.

NEEDLES

Set of 5 size 3 mm (no exact U.S. equivalent; between U.S. sizes 2 and 3) double-pointed needles (dpn). Adjust needle size if necessary to obtain the correct gauge.

NOTIONS

Marker (m), tapestry needle.

GAUGE

23 sts and 30 rows = 4" (10 cm) in chart patt worked in rounds.

SWEATER

BODY

With cir needle and B, CO 83 (89, 95, 101, 107) sts place marker (pm) for side, CO 83 (89, 95, 101, 107) sts using cable method—166 (178, 190, 202, 214) sts. Pm for beg of rnd and join for working in rnds.

Knit 19 rnds.

Work Border 1 section of Body chart as foll: *beg at right-hand edge of chart, knit first st, beg at your size and work 0 (3, 6, 9, 12) sts, work 36-st rep twice, work next 9 (12, 15, 18, 21) sts, work last st of chart; rep from * once more.

Cont Rnds 2–39 as established.

Work in Main Patt section of Body chart until piece measures about 9½ (10, 10½, 11½, 12)" (24 [25.5, 26.5, 29, 30.5] cm) from beg.

FRONT

Work first 83 (89, 95, 101, 107) sts, place rem 83 (89, 95, 101, 107) sts on holder or waste yarn for back. Cont Main Patt section of Body chart back and forth until armhole measures 3¾ (4, 4, 4, 4¼)" (9.5 [10, 10, 10, 11] cm), ending with a WS row.

Shape Neck

Next row (RS): Work 24 (26, 29, 31, 34) sts, place rem 59 (63, 66, 70, 73) sts on holder or waste yarn.

Next row (WS): Work in patt as established.

Next (dec) row: Work to last 3 sts, ssk, k1—1 st dec'd.

Next row: Purl in patt to end.

Rep last 2 rows twice more—21 (23, 26, 28, 31) sts rem. At the same time, when armhole measures about 4½ (4¾, 5, 5½, 5¾)" (11.5 [12, 12.5, 14, 14.5] cm), end with Row 45, 51, or 57 of patt chart.

Work Border 2 section of Body chart. Place sts on holder.

Return last 24 (26, 29, 31, 34) sts to needle, leaving center 35 (37, 37, 39, 39) sts on holder or waste yarn. Join yarn to beg with a RS row.

Work 2 rows even.

Next (dec) row (RS): K1, k2tog, work to end—1 st dec'd.

Next row (WS): Work in patt as established.

Rep last 2 rows twice more—21 (23, 26, 28, 31) sts rem. At the same time, when armhole measures about 4½ (4¾, 5, 5½, 5¾)" (11.5 [12, 12.5, 14, 14.5] cm), end with Row 45, 51, or 57 of patt chart.

Work Border 2 section of Body chart. Place sts on holder.

BACK

Return rem 83 (89, 95, 101, 107) sts to cir needle. Cont Main Patt section of Body chart back and forth until armhole measures 4¼ (4½, 4¾, 5¼, 6½)" (11 [11.5, 12, 13.5, 16.5] cm), ending with a WS row.

Shape Neck

Next row (RS): Work 23 (25, 28, 30, 33) sts, place rem 60 (64, 67, 71, 74) sts on holder or waste yarn.

Next row (WS): Work in patt as established.

Next (dec) row: Work to last 3 sts, ssk, k1—1 st dec'd.

Next row: Purl in patt to end.

Rep last 2 rows once more—21 (23, 26, 28, 31) sts rem. At the same time, when armhole measures about 4½ (4¾, 5, 5½, 5¾)" (11.5 [12, 12.5, 14, 14.5] cm), end with Row 45, 51, or 57 of patt chart.

Work Border 2 section of Body chart. Place sts on holder.

Return last 23 (25, 28, 30, 33) sts to needle, leaving center 37 (39, 39, 41, 41) sts on holder or waste yarn. Join yarn to beg with a RS row.

Work 2 rows even.

Next (dec) row (RS): K1, k2tog, work to end—1 st dec'd.

Body

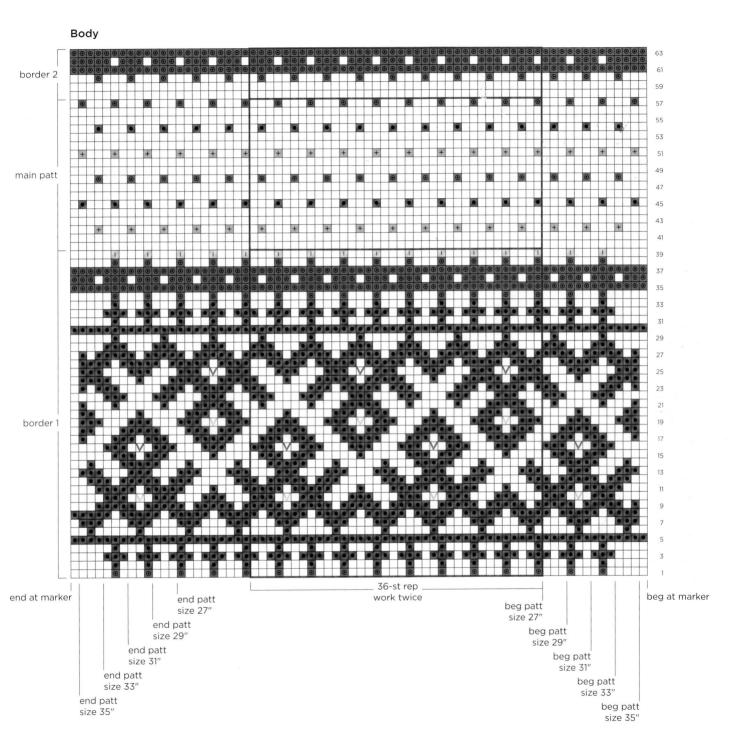

border 2

main patt

border 1

end at marker

end patt
size 35"

end patt
size 33"

end patt
size 31"

end patt
size 29"

end patt
size 27"

36-st rep
work twice

beg patt
size 27"

beg patt
size 29"

beg patt
size 31"

beg patt
size 33"

beg patt
size 35"

beg at marker

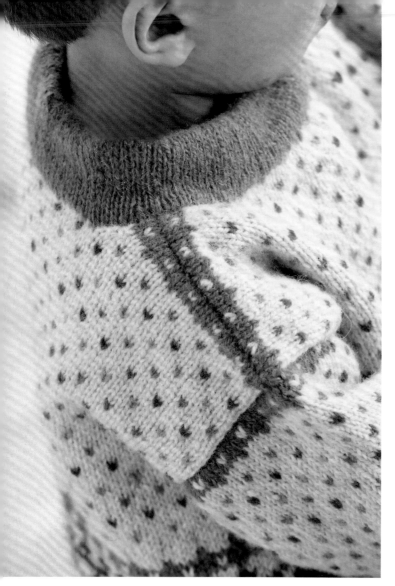

Next row (WS): Work in patt as established.

Rep last 2 rows once more—21 (23, 26, 28, 31) sts rem. At the same time, when armhole measures about 4½ (4¾, 5, 5½, 5¾)" (11.5 [12, 12.5, 14, 14.5] cm), end with Row 45, 51, or 57 of patt chart.

Work Border 2 section of Body chart. Place sts on holder.

Join Shoulders

Return held left shoulder sts to dpn. Hold needles with RS tog, join sts using three-needle BO. Rep with right shoulder sts.

SLEEVE (MAKE 2)

With dpn and B, CO 40 (42, 44, 46, 48) sts using cable method. Pm for beg of rnd and join for working in rnds.

Knit 20 rnds.

Work Border 3 section of Sleeve chart as foll: beg at right-hand edge of chart, knit first st, beg at your size and work 3 (4, 5, 6, 7) sts, work 4-st rep 8 times, work next 3 (4, 5, 6, 7) sts, work last st of chart.

Cont Rnds 2–10 as established, then work in Main Patt section of Sleeve chart until piece measures about 9½ (10, 10½, 11½, 12)" (24 [25.5, 26.5, 29, 30.5] cm) from beg. At the same time, inc 1 st each end every other rnd 5 times, every 4 rnds 4 times, then every 6 rnds 3 (4, 5, 6, 7) times—64 (68, 72, 76, 80) sts. Work inc sts into patt.

Work even until piece measures 10¾ (11¼, 11¾, 12¾, 14¼)" (27.5 [28.5, 30, 32.5, 36] cm) from beg, ending with Rnd 16, 22, or 28 of patt chart.

Work Border 2 section of Sleeve chart.

Join Sleeve to Body

With dpn and B, with RS facing, beg at bottom of armhole, pick up and knit 64 (68, 72, 76, 80) sts evenly along armhole edge.

Turn body with WS facing. Place sleeve inside with RS of both pieces held tog and beg of sleeve rnds at bottom of armhole. Join sleeve to body using three-needle BO.

Neckband

With dpn, B, and with RS facing, pick up and knit 10 (10, 11, 12, 12) sts along left front neck edge, knit 35 (37, 37, 39, 39) sts from front holder, pick up and knit 17 (17, 18, 19, 19) sts along left neck edge, knit 37 (39, 39, 41, 41) sts from back holder, then pick up and knit 7 sts along left back neck edge—106 (110, 112, 118, 118) sts. Pm for beg of rnd and join for working in rnds.

Rnd 1 (dec): K9 (10, 11, 12, 12), ssk, k5, ssk, k3, ssk, k5, k2tog, k3, k2tog, k5, k2tog, k3, k2tog, k14 (16, 17, 19, 19), ssk, k9, ssk, k5, ssk, k6, k2tog, k9, k2tog, k6 (7, 8, 10, 10)—94 (98, 100, 106, 106) sts rem.

Rnd 2 (dec): (Ssk, k21 [22, 22, 24, 24]) 2 times, k2tog, (ssk, k20 [21, 22, 23, 23]) 2 times, k2tog—88 (92, 94, 100, 100) sts rem.

Rnds 3–13: Knit.

Rnd 14 (dec): *K7, ssk; rep from * 8 (9, 9, 10, 10) more times, knit to end—79 (82, 84, 89, 89) sts rem.

Rnds 15–23: Knit.

BO all sts very loosely.

FINISHING

Work duplicate st foll chart.

Weave in all ends.

Turn CO edge of body to inside and sew edge to last rnd of B for hem. Rep with sleeves. Turn BO edge of neckband to inside and sew loosely to neck edge.

Handwash in warm soapy water and carefully roll up in a towel and gently squeeze out excess water. Reshape and leave to dry flat away from sun or direct heat.

Press very lightly with a warm iron over a damp cloth.

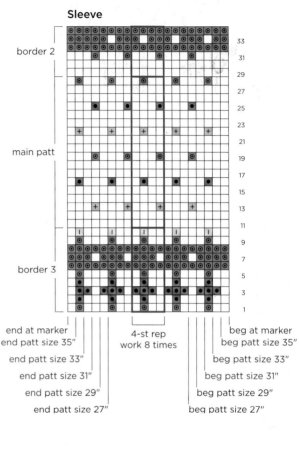

Sleeve

border 2

main patt

border 3

end at marker
end patt size 35"

end patt size 33"

end patt size 31"

end patt size 29"

end patt size 27"

4-st rep
work 8 times

beg at marker
beg patt size 35"

beg patt size 33"

beg patt size 31"

beg patt size 29"

beg patt size 27"

☐ natural beige

◉ soft blue

● soft red

+ light orange

I soft yellow

V knit with natural beige, duplicate st with soft blue

V knit with natural beige, duplicate st with soft yellow

☐ pattern repeat

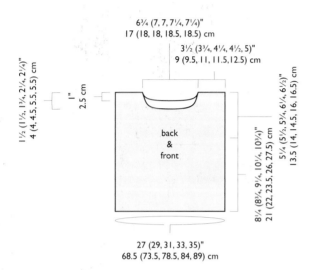

6¾ (7, 7, 7¼, 7¼)"
17 (18, 18, 18.5, 18.5) cm

3½ (3¾, 4¼, 4½, 5)"
9 (9.5, 11, 11.5,12.5) cm

1½ (1½, 1¾, 2¼, 2¼)"
4 (4,4.5,5.5,5.5) cm

1"
2.5 cm

back
&
front

5¼ (5½, 5¾, 6¼, 6½)"
13.5 (14, 14.5, 16, 16.5) cm

8¼ (8¾, 9¼, 10¼, 10¾)"
21 (22, 23.5, 26, 27.5) cm

27 (29, 31, 33, 35)"
68.5 (73.5, 78.5, 84, 89) cm

10½ (11, 11¾, 12½, 13)"
26.5 (28, 30, 31.5, 33) cm

sleeve

10¼ (10¾, 11¼, 12¼, 13¾)"
26 (27.5, 28.5, 31, 35) cm

6½ (7, 7¼, 7½, 7¾)"
16.5 (18, 18.5, 19, 19.5) cm

HAT

With C, CO 111 sts using the cable method. Place marker (pm) for beg of rnd and join for working in rounds.

Knit 19 rnds.

Change to A. Knit 1 rnd.

Beg Main Patt chart, working as foll: Work first st of chart, work 36-st rep 3 times, work rem 2 sts.

Cont as established through Rnd 31.

Rnd 32 (dec): K2tog, work chart as established to last 2 sts, ssk—2 sts dec'd.

Rnd 33 (dec): Sl first st, work to last st, sl last st, remove m, knit first st of rnd, psso, replace m—108 sts rem.

Work Lice Stitch chart Rnds 1–18 once, then Rnds 1–6 once more. Cut yarn.

Distribute sts over 2 dpn as foll: first 27 and last 27 sts on Needle 1, then rem 54 sts on Needle 2.

Turn piece with WS facing. Attach yarn at one end and join sts using three-needle BO.

FINISHING

Work duplicate st foll chart.

Turn CO edge to WS and sew edge to last rnd of C for hem.

Weave in all ends.

I-Cord

With B, CO 2 sts.

Row 1: Knit. Slide sts back to right end of needle and do not turn.

Row 2: Pull yarn across back of work, k2. Slide sts back to right end of needle and do not turn.

Rep Row 2 until I-cord measures about 9" (23 cm), or desired length. BO all sts.

Lice Stitch

	A
o (B symbol)	B
+ (C symbol)	C
I (D symbol)	D
/	k2tog
\	ssk
	no stitch
V	knit with B, duplicate st with C

Main Patt

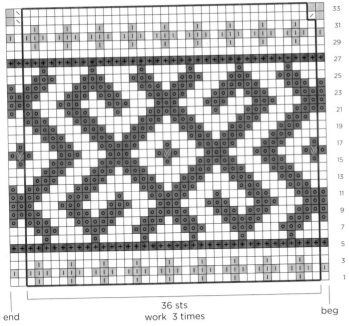

36 sts
work 3 times

end   beg

Thread cord through corners at top edge.

With B, make 2 tassels, each about 2" (5 cm) long.
Attach tassels to each end of I-cord.

Handwash in warm soapy water and carefully roll up in a towel
and gently squeeze out excess water. Reshape and leave to
dry flat away from sun or heat source.

Press very lightly with a warm iron over a damp cloth.

Pull corners to back of hat and knot I-cord next to corners.

Tovio Mittens and Hat

FINLAND

There is a strong sense of East meets West when you study traditional Finnish knitted designs: the yarns are often stronger and brighter than those of its other Nordic neighbors, there is a tradition for using a lot of black and white together, and some of the patterns are influenced by Eastern motifs. The Tovio Mittens and Hat exhibit many of these characteristics, knitted in the round using the stranded, or Fair Isle, technique.

MITTENS

FINISHED SIZE
Hand circumference 7¾" (19.5 cm).

Length 10½" (26.5 cm).

YARN
Fingering Weight (#1 Super Fine).

Shown here: Riihivila Aarni (100% wool; 131 yd [120 m]/3½ oz [100 g]): #1205 natural black (A), 2 skeins; #1006 natural beige (B), 1 skein; #3384 soft red (C), 1 skein; #3305 yellow (D), 1 skein.

NEEDLES
Set of 5 size 3 mm (no exact U.S. equivalent; between U.S. sizes 2 and 3) double-pointed (dpn). Adjust needle size if necessary to obtain the correct gauge.

Set of 5 size U.S. 2 (2.75 mm) double-pointed (dpn).

NOTIONS
Marker (m), holder or waste yarn, tapestry needle.

GAUGE
26 sts and 29 rows = 4" (10 cm) over chart using larger needles worked in rnds.

HAT

FINISHED SIZE
Circumference 18¼" (46.5 cm).

YARN
Fingering weight (#1 Super Fine).

Shown here: Riihivila Aarni (100% wool; 131 yd [120 m]/3½ oz [100 g]): #1205 natural black (A), 2 skeins; #1006 natural beige (B), 1 skein; #3384 soft red (C), 1 skein; #3305 yellow (D), 1 skein.

NEEDLES
Set of 5 size 3 mm (no exact U.S. equivalent; between U.S. sizes 2 and 3) double-pointed (dpn). Adjust needle size if necessary to obtain the correct gauge.

Set of 5 size 2.5 mm (no exact U.S. equivalent; between U.S. sizes 1 and 2) double-pointed (dpn).

Set of 5 size U.S. 1 (2.25 mm) double-pointed (dpn).

NOTIONS
Marker (m), tapestry needle.

GAUGE
28 sts and 35 rows = 4" (10 cm) over rib using largest needles worked in rnds.

MITTENS

RIGHT MITTEN

Using A and smaller dpn, CO 48 sts. Place marker (pm) and join for working in rnds. Divide sts evenly over 4 dpn (12 sts on each needle).

Change to larger dpn. Work 8 rnds of k2, p2 rib.

Work Hand chart to Row 31—50 sts.

Thumbhole

Next rnd: Work 26 sts, place next 9 sts on holder or waste yarn, CO 9 sts using backward-loop method, work to end.

Cont working through chart Row 59.

Shape Top

Arrange sts if necessary with 13 sts each on Needles 1 and 3 and 12 sts each on Needles 2 and 4.

Shape top foll Rows 60–69 of chart—10 sts rem.

Cut yarn, leaving an 8" (20.5 cm) tail, thread tail through rem sts, pull tight to close hole, and fasten off on WS.

Thumb

Place 9 sts from holder on larger dpn, pick up and k9 sts along CO sts above thumb opening—18 sts. Arrange sts evenly over 4 dpn. Pm and join for working in rnds.

Work Thumb chart. Arrange sts if necessary with 4 sts each on Needles 1 and 3 and 5 sts each on Needles 2 and 4.

Shape Top

Next rnd (dec): With C, *k1, k2tog tbl, k3, k2tog, k1; rep from * once more—14 sts.

Next rnd (dec): *K1, k2tog tbl, k1, k2tog, k1; rep from * once more—10 sts.

Cut yarn, leaving an 8" (20.5 cm) tail, thread tail through rem sts, pull tight to close hole, and fasten off on WS.

Hand

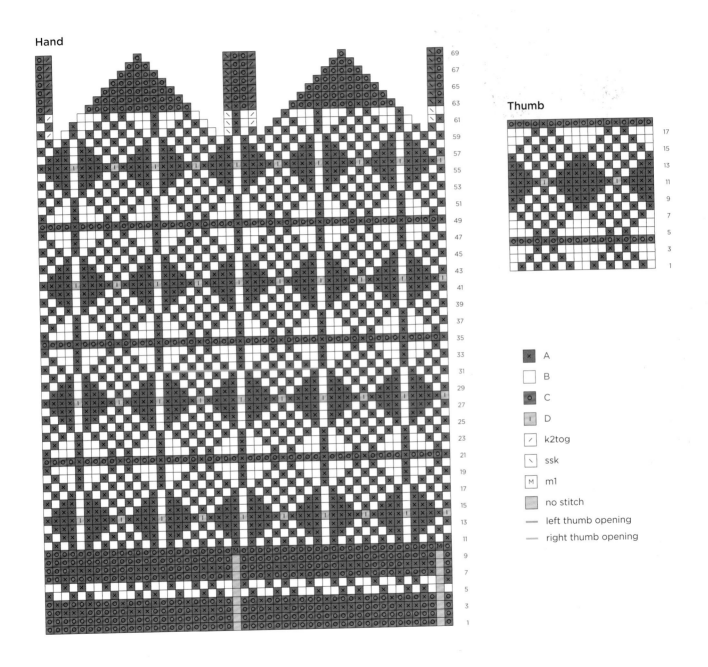

Thumb

- ⬛ A
- ⬜ B
- ◉ C
- I D
- ╱ k2tog
- ╲ ssk
- M m1
- ▨ no stitch
- — left thumb opening
- — right thumb opening

LEFT MITTEN

Work hand same as right mitten to Row 31 of Hand chart.

Thumbhole

Next rnd: Work 16 sts, place next 9 sts on holder or waste yarn, CO 9 sts using backward-loop method, work to end.

Cont same as right mitten.

FINISHING

Weave in ends.

Handwash in warm soapy water and carefully roll up in a towel and gently squeeze out excess water.

Reshape and leave to dry flat away from sun or heat source.

Press very lightly with a warm iron over a damp cloth.

HAT

With A and size 3 mm dpn, CO 128 sts using the cable method. Place marker (pm) and join for working in rnds. Divide sts evenly over 4 dpn.

Work 6 rnds of k2, p2 rib.

Next rnd: Join C and knit.

Next rnd (inc): K1, m1, k64, m1, knit to end—130 sts.

Work Rows 1–21 of Hat chart.

Change to C. Knit 2 rnds. Change to A. Knit 1 rnd.

Next rnd (inc): *K2tog, k1, (p2, k2) 15 times, p2; rep from * once more—128 sts.

Work even in rib until piece measures about 10¼" (26 cm) from beg, or desired length.

Hat

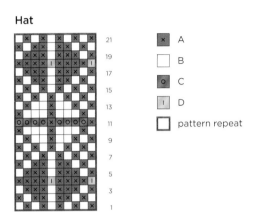

		A
		B
		C
		D
		pattern repeat

Shape Top

Change to size 2.5 mm dpn. Work 6 rnds of rib.

Change to size 1 (2.25 mm) dpn. Work 10 rnds of rib.

Next rnd (dec): *K2, p2tog; rep from *—96 sts rem.

Turn piece with WS facing.

Next rnd (dec): *Ssk; rep from *—48 sts rem.

Rep dec rnd once more—24 sts rem.

Cut yarn, leaving an 8" (20.5 cm) tail, thread tail through rem sts, pull tight to close hole, and fasten off on WS.

FINISHING

Weave in all yarn ends.

Handwash in warm soapy water and carefully roll up in a towel and gently squeeze out excess water.

Reshape and leave to dry flat away from sun or heat source.

Press very lightly with a warm iron over a damp cloth.

With C, make a large pom-pom, about 3" (7.5 cm) diameter. Attach pom-pom to top of hat.

Adda Socks

DENMARK

Damask knitting has been popular in Denmark since at least the eighteenth century, and in common with many traditional knitting techniques and patterns at that time, probably was developed to imitate woven fabrics and motifs. The technique, in which patterns of purl stitches were knitted in relief on a stockinette background, was usually made using exceptionally thin yarn on fine needles, yielding a fabric with a very high stitch count. In an attempt to copy the exquisitely patterned silk blouses popular with the upper classes, women of the lower classes would knit Damask sleeves and attach them to fabric bodices. These sleeves, as well as entire nightshirts, would be knitted in fine red, green, or black colored yarn and patterned all over with flowers, birds, and animal shapes, but most commonly star motifs.

Inspired by this traditional technique, these simple Adda socks have large Damask patterned stars with embroidered detailing.

I have chosen to use the fine wool yarn doubled, as it will create a more substantial gauge ideal for a thicker, more cozy house or lounging socks.

FINISHED MEASUREMENTS
8" (20.5 cm) foot circumference and 8" (20.5 cm) long.

YARN
Fingering weight (#1 Super Fine).

Shown here: Isager Tvinni (100% merino wool; 280 yd [256 m]/50 g): #40 chartreuse (A), 1 skein; #15 dark chartreuse (B), 1 skein; #15s dark chartreuse on gray (C), 1 skein.

NEEDLES
Set of 5 size 5 (3.75 mm) double-pointed needles (dpn). Adjust needle size if necessary to obtain the correct gauge.

NOTIONS
Marker (m), tapestry needle.

GAUGE
24 sts and 37 rnds = 4" (10 cm) with yarn held double in St st worked in rounds.

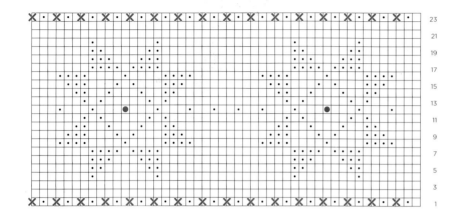

		knit
	·	purl
	●	knit with A, French knot with B
	X	cross-st with B, centered between 2 sts; last cross-st is worked over last st and first st of rnd.

SOCKS

With 2 strands of A, CO 48 sts using the cable method. Place marker (pm) for beg of rnd and join for working in rnds.

Rnd 1: *K2, p2; rep from * around.

Rep last rnd 25 more times.

Knit 3 rnds.

Work chart rnds 1—23. Knit 3 rnds.

Cut both strands of A and join 2 strands of B. Knit 2 rnds.

Heel

Row 1: K12, turn.

Row 2 (WS): Sl 1, p23, turn; leave rem 24 sts on separate dpn. Cont back and forth on the 24 heel sts.

Row 3 (RS): Sl 1, knit to end of row.

Row 4: Sl 1, purl to end of row.

Rep Rows 3 and 4 eight more times; heel should measure about 1¾" (4.5 cm).

Shape Heel

Row 1: K14, skp, k1, turn.

Row 2: Sl 1, p5, p2tog, p1, turn.

Row 3: Sl 1, k6, skp, k1, turn.

Row 4: Sl 1, p7, p2tog, p1, turn.

Row 5: Sl 1, k8, skp, k1, turn.

Row 6: Sl 1, p9, p2tog, p1, turn.

Row 7: Sl 1, k10, skp, k1, turn.

Row 8: Sl 1, p11, p2tog, p1, turn.

Row 9: Skp, knit to the end, turn.

Row 10: P2tog, purl to the end, turn—14 sts rem.

Gusset

Needle 4, K7 heel sts; Needle 1, knit rem 7 heel sts, pick up and k12 sts along side edge of heel; Needles 2 and 3, knit across the held 24 instep sts; Needle 4, pick up and knit 12 sts along rem edge of heel, knit 7 heel sts—62 sts.

Distribute sts if necessary with 19 sts (7 heel sts and 12 gusset sts) each on Needles 1 and 4 and 12 instep sts each on Needles 2 and 3. Pm for beg of rnd and join for working in rnds; rnds start at back of heel.

Next (dec) rnd: Needle 1, knit to last 3 sts k2tog, k1; Needles 2 and 3, knit; Needle 4, k1, ssk, knit to end—2 sts dec'd.

Next rnd: Knit.

Rep last 2 rnds 6 more times—48 sts rem; 12 sts on each needle.

Foot

Knit 17 rnds even.

Cut both strands of B and join 2 strands of C. Knit 10 rnds; foot should measure about 6″ (15 cm) from heel.

Wedge Toe Shaping

Next (dec) rnd: Needle 1, knit to last 3 sts, k2tog, k1; Needle 2, k1, ssk, knit to end; Needle 3, knit to last 3 sts, k2tog, k1; Needle 4, k1, ssk, knit to end—4 sts dec'd.

Next rnd: Knit.

Rep last 2 rnds 8 more times—8 sts rem.

Cut yarn, leaving an 8″ (20.5 cm) tail, thread tail through rem sts, pull tight to close hole, and fasten off on WS.

FINISHING

Weave in all ends.

Work embroidery foll chart.

Turn half of rib to inside to form cuff and stitch to WS.

Handwash in warm soapy water and carefully roll up in a towel and gently squeeze out excess water. Reshape and leave unpinned or stretched to dry flat away from sun or heat source.

Press very lightly with a warm iron over a damp cloth.

Rya Flower Cushion

DENMARK

This quirky, fun flower cushion will make a wonderful gift and addition to any home. It has been inspired by two traditional Danish textile techniques: the beautiful Danish whitework known as Hedebo, and the traditional, decorative Danish wool rya. Hedebo is a specific type of cut and drawn work on white linen that was used as decoration for household linens. Originally made by peasants using patterns inspired by the natural world and other decorative folk craft, the early patterns depicted large stylized foliate and floral shapes.

This Rya Flower Cushion is knitted in the round, with two separate leaves and one stem. Purl stitches are used as outlines for the patterned areas, and once the knitting is completed, the rya tufts are hooked through the front of the knitting and trimmed. Simple French knots are used as further decoration.

FINISHED SIZE
22" (56 cm) circumference and 13" (33 cm) tall.

YARN
Laceweight (#0 Lace).

Shown here: Isager Spinni (100% wool; 340 yd [311 m]/1¾ oz [50 g]): #0 natural white (A), 4 skeins; #47 steel gray (B), 1 skein; #16 marine blue green (C), 1 skein; #40 chartreuse (D), 1 skein; #10s light blue green (E), 1 skein.

NEEDLES
Size 3 mm (no exact U.S. equivalent; between U.S. sizes 2 and 3) 24" (60 cm) circular (cir) and set of 5 double-pointed needles (dpn). Adjust needle size if necessary to obtain the correct gauge.

Size 3 mm (no exact U.S. equivalent; between U.S. sizes C/2 and D/3) crochet hook.

Size 1 (2 mm) crochet hook.

NOTIONS
Markers (m), locking markers, fleece or fiberfill, tapestry needle.

GAUGE
25 sts and 34 rnds = 4" (10 cm) in St st, worked in rounds with yarn held double.

CUSHION

With 2 strands of A and cir needle, CO 104 sts using the cable cast on method. Place marker (pm) and join for working in rnds. Place center m after 52 sts and locking marker on sts 26 and 78 to mark for placing the stem.

Rnd 1: K2, m1 using bar increase, knit to 2 sts before center m, m1, k4, m1, knit to 2 sts before end of rnd m, m1, k2—4 sts inc'd.

Rep Rnd 1 ten more times—148 sts.

Next rnd: Work Rnd 1 of Flower chart to center m, knit to end.

Work Rnds 2–72 of Flower chart as established; piece should measure about 9¾" (25 cm) from beg.

Petals

Work each petal individually using dpn.

First Petal: K24, slip next 100 sts on holders, knit rem 24 sts—48 sts.

Divide sts evenly over 4 dpn (12 sts on each needle). Pm for beg of rnd, keeping the beg of rnd at the outside edge.

Work Rnd 74 over first 24 sts, knit to end.

Work Rnds 75–87 as established.

Shape Top

Next (dec) rnd: *K4, k2tog; rep from * around—40 sts rem.

Knit 2 rnds even.

Next (dec) rnd: *K3, k2tog; rep from * around—32 sts rem.

Knit 2 rnds even.

Next (dec) rnd: *K2, k2tog; rep from * around—24 sts rem.

Knit 1 rnd even.

Next (dec) rnd: *K1, k2tog; rep from * around—16 sts rem.

Next (dec) rnd: *K2tog; rep from * around—8 sts rem.

Cut yarn, thread tail through rem sts, pull tight to close hole, and fasten off on WS.

Second Petal: Place first 25 sts and last 25 sts on dpn—50 sts,

Leaf

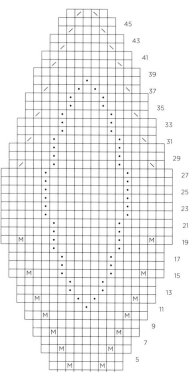

knit
· purl
/ k2tog
\ ssk
M m1
no stitch

and 50 sts rem on holders. Pm for beg of rnd and join for working in rnds.

Next (dec) rnd: Work Rnd 74 of chart over next 25 sts, knit to last 2 sts, k2tog—48 sts.

Work Rnds 75–87 as established. Shape top same as first petal.

Third Petal: Place rem 50 sts on dpn. Pm for beg of rnd and join for working in rnds.

Next (dec) rnd: Work Rnd 74 of chart over next 25 sts, knit to last 2 sts, ssk—48 sts.

Work Rnds 75–87 as established. Shape top same as first petal.

Leaves (make 2)

With 2 strands of A and dpn, CO 10 sts using the cable method. Pm for beg of rnd and join for working in rnds. Pm second m for center of rnd.

Rnd 1: Work Row 1 of Leaf chart over first 5 sts, knit to end.

Rnd 2: Work Row 2 of Leaf chart over first 5 sts, plus 2 inc sts, k2, m1, knit to 2 sts before m, m1, k2—4 sts inc'd.

Work Rnds 3–46 of Leaf chart as established—10 sts rem.

Cut yarn, leaving an 8" (20.5 cm) tail, thread tail through rem sts but do not pull tight to leave open for stuffing.

Stem

With 2 strands of A and dpn, CO 22 sts using the cable method, leaving a 12" (30.5 cm) tail for joining stem to main flower. Pm for beg of rnd and join for working in rnds.

Knit 25 rnds even.

Shape End

Next (dec) rnd: *K1, k2tog; rep from * to last st, k1—17 sts rem.

Next (dec) rnd: *K2tog; rep from * around—9 sts rem.

Rep last rnd once more—5 sts rem.

Cut yarn, leaving an 8" (20.5 cm) tail, thread tail through rem sts, pull tight to close hole, and fasten off on WS.

Fringe

A basic fringe is made by winding the yarn around a 2¼" (5.5 cm) piece of cardboard 5 times. Carefully slip the wound yarn from the card.

Always working with RS facing, use the purl stitches as a guide, pass the smaller crochet hook behind a purl stitch (passing it from the front under the stitch and then up behind the stitch to the front again).

Catch the tops of the looped yarn with the crochet hook and pull through the end of the looped yarn behind the stitch, to the RS, leaving a large loop on the bottom. Remove smaller hook.

Flower

87
85
83
81
79
77
75
73
71
69
67
65
63
61
59
57
55
53
51
49
47
45
43
41
39
37
35
33
31
29
27
25
23
21
19
17
15
13
11
9
7
5
3
1

Using larger crochet hook, catch the lower loops of fringe yarn and pull through the smaller top loops; pull tight to secure and form a knot.

One rya fringe has been made.

Cont making fringe in each purl stitch.

When all fringes are complete, trim to about 1" (2.5 cm) long; I would recommend using two pieces of cardboard as a guide. Catch the fringe between the cards, then trim.

FINISHING

Using photo as a guide, randomly work small French knots in center of each circle.

Weave in all ends.

Handwash in warm soapy water and carefully roll up in a towel and gently squeeze out any excess water.

Reshape and leave to dry flat away from sun or heat source.

Press and block carefully with a warm iron over a damp cloth.

Fill main flower, petals, leaves, and stem with fleece or fiberfill. Pull yarn to close rem opening in each leaf and fasten off and pull yarn inside leaf. Sew CO edge of stem closed.

Pin stem to bottom edges of main flower, centering locking m on each side of stem. Sew CO edge of flower closed, sewing through all layers of stem. Sew straight side edge of each leaf to bottom of main flower so one end touches stem. Sew end of each leaf to stem.

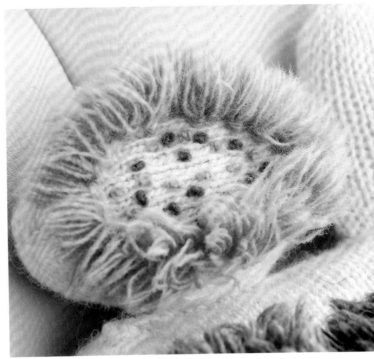

Glossary

Abbreviations

beg(s)	begin(s); beginning
BO	bind off
CC	contrasting color
cm	centimeter(s)
cn	cable needle
CO	cast on
cont	continue(s); continuing
dec(s)	decrease(s); decreasing
dpn	double-pointed needles
foll	follow(s); following
g	gram(s)
inc(s)	increase(s); increasing
k	knit
k1-b	knit into the back loop of a stitch
k1f&b	knit into the front and back of same stitch
kwise	knitwise, as if to knit
m	marker(s)
MC	main color
mm	millimeter(s)
M1	make one (increase)
p	purl
p1f&b	purl into front and back of same stitch
patt(s)	pattern(s)
psso	pass slipped stitch over
pwise	purlwise, as if to purl
rem	remain(s); remaining

rep	repeat(s); repeating
rev St st	reverse stockinette stitch
rnd(s)	round(s)
RS	right side
skp	slip a stitch, knit the next stitch, pass the slipped stitch over
sl	slip
sl st	slip st (slip 1 stitch purlwise unless otherwise indicated)
sm	slip marker
ssk	slip 2 stitches knitwise, one at a time, from the left needle to right needle, insert left needle tip through both front loops and knit together from this position (1 stitch decrease)
st(s)	stitch(es)
St st	stockinette stitch
tbl	through back loop
tog	together
WS	wrong side
wyb	with yarn in back
wyf	with yarn in front
yd	yard(s)
yo	yarnover
*	repeat starting point
* *	repeat all instructions between asterisks
( )	alternate measurements and/or instructions
[ ]	work instructions as a group a specified number of times

Cast-Ons

BACKWARD-LOOP CAST-ON

*Loop working yarn and place it on needle backward so that it doesn't unwind. Repeat from *.

CABLE CAST-ON

If there are no stitches on the needle, make a slipknot of working yarn and place it on the needle, then use the knitted method to cast-on one more stitch—two stitches on needle. Hold needle with working yarn in your left hand with the wrong side of the work facing you. *Insert right needle *between* the first two stitches on left needle **(Figure 1)**, wrap yarn around needle as if to knit, draw yarn through **(Figure 2)**, and place new loop on left needle **(Figure 3)** to form a new stitch. Repeat from * for the desired number of stitches, always working between the first two stitches on the left needle.

Figure 1

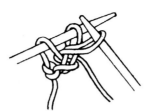

Figure 2

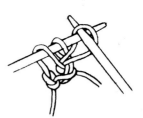

Figure 3

TWINED CAST-ON

Leaving long tails for braiding later, make a slipknot with two strands of A and one strand of B held tog, and place the slipknot on the right needle; the slipknot does not count as a CO st. Hold B in your left hand and the two strands of A in your right hand (**Figure 1**). Loop B around the left thumb and insert right needle tip into the loop as if to start a long-tail cast-on (**Figure 2**), wrap one strand of A around the needle as if to knit, lift loop B over strand of A and off needle (**Figure 3**), drop the B loop from the left thumb, and tighten the new st. *Loop B around left thumb again, insert needle tip into the loop, bring the strand of A farthest from the right needle tip over the previous strand of A used, wrap it around the right needle as if to knit, lift loop B over strand of A and off needle, drop the B loop from the left thumb and tighten; rep from * until the required number of sts are CO, alternating strands of A and bringing each strand over the one used before. Break off B. Drop the slipknot from the needle before joining in the rnd, but do not untie it yet.

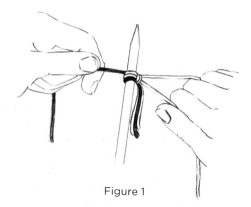

Figure 1

Figure 2

Figure 3

TWINED CAST-ON WITH DOUBLE BEAD

Leaving long tails for braiding later, make a slipknot with two strands of A and one strand of B, and place the slipknot on the needle; the slipknot does not count as a CO st. Hold B in your left hand and the needle and two strands of A in your right hand (**Figure 1**). Loop B around the left thumb. Slip the needle tip underneath both strands of the loop, between the loop and the web of your thumb (and not into the loop itself yet). Next, insert the needle tip down into the thumb loop from top to bottom (**Figure 2**) and rotate the needle so its tip is pointing upward again—the thumb loop now forms a figure eight, with the thumb and needle in separate compartments of the eight (**Figure 3**). Wrap one strand of A around the needle as if to knit.

Insert the needle tip up into the thumb loop from bottom to top (**Figure 4**; this will undo the twist of the figure eight), drop the B loop from the left thumb, and tighten the new st.*Loop B around left thumb again, slip needle tip underneath both strands of the loop, then insert it down into the thumb loop from top to bottom. Rotate the needle so its tip is pointing upward again, bring the strand of A farthest from the needle tip over the previous strand of A used, and wrap it around the needle as if to knit. Insert the needle tip up into the thumb loop from bottom to top, drop the B loop from the left thumb, and tighten the new st; rep from * until the required number of sts are CO, alternating strands of A and bringing each strand over the one used before. Break off B. Drop the slipknot from the needle before joining in the rnd but do not untie it yet.

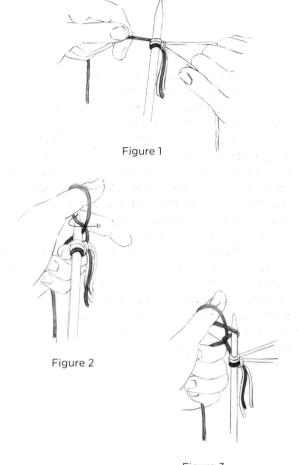

Figure 1

Figure 2

Figure 3

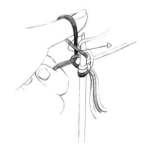

Figure 4

Bind-Off

THREE-NEEDLE BIND-OFF

Place the stitches to be joined onto two separate needles and hold the needles parallel so that the two sides of knitting face together. Insert a third needle into the first stitch on each of two needles **(Figure 1)** and knit them together as one stitch **(Figure 2)**, *knit the next stitch on each needle the same way, then use the left needle tip to lift the first stitch over the second and off the needle **(Figure 3)**. Repeat from * until no stitches remain on first two needles. Cut yarn and pull tail through last stitch to secure.

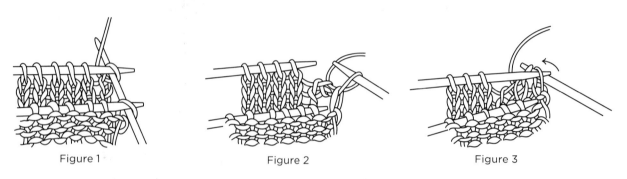

Figure 1   Figure 2   Figure 3

Crochet

SINGLE CROCHET

*Insert hook in stitch, yarn over and pull up loop **(Figure 1)**, yarn over and draw through both loops on the hook **(Figure 2)**; repeat from *.

Figure 1

Figure 2

Embroidery

CROSS-STITCH

Bring threaded needle out from back to front at lower left edge of the knitted stitch (or stitches) to be covered. Working from left to right, *insert needle at the upper right edges of the same stitch(es) and bring it back out at the lower left edge of the adjacent stitch, directly below and in line with the insertion point. Work from right to left to work the other half of the cross.

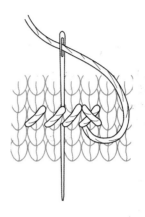

BULLION STITCH

Bring threaded needle out of knitted background from back to front. Insert needle a measure of distance away (the length of your bullion) and bring it back up at the starting point. Wrap thread around the needle a number of times as desired. Pull the needle through in an upward direction, adjusting the wraps as necessary. Re-insert the needle at the other entry point to tack down the bullion.

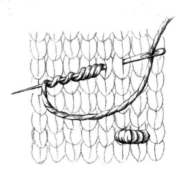

STRAIGHT STITCH

Bring threaded needle in and out of background to form a dashed line.

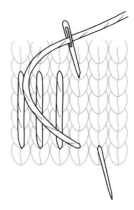

FRENCH KNOT

Bring threaded needle out of knitted background from back to front, wrap yarn around needle three times, and use your thumb to hold the wraps in place while you insert the needle into the background a short distance from where it came out. Pull the needle through the wraps into the background.

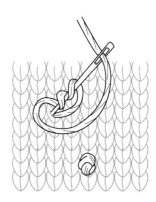

DUPLICATE STITCH

Bring threaded needle out from back to front at the base of the V of the knitted stitch you want to cover. *Working right to left, pass needle in and out under the stitch in the row above it and back into the base of the same stitch. Bring needle back out at the base of the V of the next stitch to the left. Repeat from * for desired number of stitches.

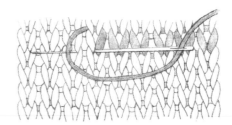

Increases

BAR INCREASE: K1F&B

Knit into a stitch but leave it on the left needle **(Figure 1)**, then knit through the back loop of the same stitch **(Figure 2)** and slip the original stitch off the needle **(Figure 3)**.

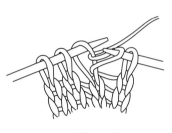

Figure 1

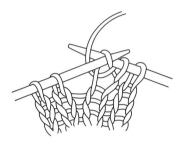

Figure 2

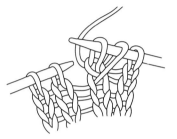

Figure 3

RAISED MAKE-ONE

NOTE: Use the left slant if no direction of slant is specified.

Left Slant (M1L)

With left needle tip, lift the strand between the last knitted stitch and the first stitch on the left needle from front to back **(Figure 1)**, then knit the lifted loop through the back **(Figure 2)**.

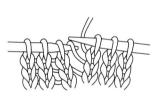

Figure 1

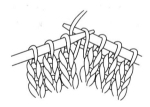

Figure 2

Right Slant (M1R)

With left needle tip, lift the strand between the needles from back to front **(Figure 1)**. Knit the lifted loop through the front **(Figure 2)**.

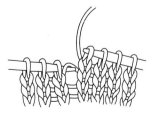

Figure 1

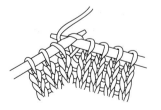

Figure 2

Grafting
KITCHENER STITCH

Arrange stitches on two needles so that there is the same number of stitches on each needle. Hold the needles parallel to each other with wrong sides of the knitting together. Allowing about ½" (1.3 cm) per stitch to be grafted, thread matching yarn on a tapestry needle. Work from right to left as follows:

STEP 1 Bring tapestry needle through the first stitch on the front needle as if to purl and leave the stitch on the needle **(Figure 1)**.

STEP 2 Bring tapestry needle through the first stitch on the back needle as if to knit and leave that stitch on the needle **(Figure 2)**.

STEP 3 Bring tapestry needle through the first front stitch as if to knit and slip this stitch off the needle, then bring tapestry needle through the next front stitch as if to purl and leave this stitch on the needle **(Figure 3)**.

STEP 4 Bring tapestry needle through the first back stitch as if to purl and slip this stitch off the needle, then bring tapestry needle through the next back stitch as if to knit and leave this stitch on the needle **(Figure 4)**.

Repeat Steps 3 and 4 until one stitch remains on each needle, adjusting the tension to match the rest of the knitting as you go. To finish, bring tapestry needle through the front stitch as if to knit and slip this stitch off the needle, then bring tapestry needle through the back stitch as if to purl and slip this stitch off the needle.

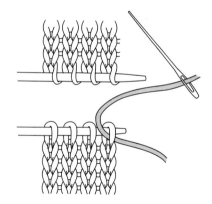

Figure 1

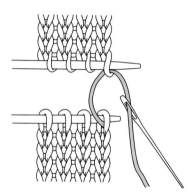

Figure 2

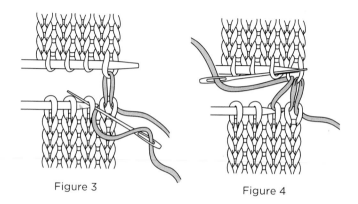

Figure 3   Figure 4

Twined Stitches

TWINED KNITTING

*With both strands in back, insert right needle into next st on left needle as if to knit, bring the strand farthest from the tip the tip of the right needle over the other strand, and use it to knit the stitch: rep from * alternating the two strands and bringing each strand over the one used before.

TWINED PURLING

*With both strands in back, insert right needle into next st on left needle as if to purl, bring the strand farthest from the tip the tip of the right needle under the other strand, and use it to purl the stitch: rep from * alternating the two strands and bringing each strand under the one used before.

Embellishments

TASSEL

Cut a piece of cardboard 4" (10 cm) wide by the desired length of the tassel plus 1" (2.5 cm). Wrap yarn to desired thickness around cardboard. Cut a short length of yarn and tie tightly around one end of wrapped yarn **(Figure 1)**. Cut yarn loops at other end. Cut another piece of yarn and wrap tightly around loops a short distance below top knot to form tassel neck. Knot securely, thread ends onto tapestry needle, and pull to center of tassel **(Figure 2)**. Trim ends.

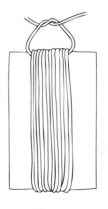

Figure 1   Figure 2

I-CORD

With double-pointed needle, cast on desired number of stitches (usually three). *Without turning the needle, slide the stitches to the other point, pull yarn around the back, and knit the stitches as usual. Repeat from * for desired length.

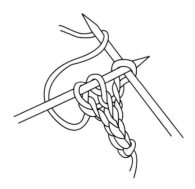

POM-POMS

Create your pom-pom template: Trace the circumference of a glass or other round object onto cardboard two times. Cut out these two circles. Trace smaller circles inside the larger circles and cut them out as well. Cut wedge openings in both discs **(Figure 1)**.

Figure 1

Cut a piece of yarn about 12" (30.5 cm) and place the end between the two pieces of cardboard. Hold the two pieces of cardboard together and begin wrapping yarn around the cardboard template. The more yarn you wrap around, then the denser your pom-pom will be. Make a loose slipknot with the tie yarn that is sandwiched between the cardboard. Slip your scissors in-between the two pieces of cardboard and begin cutting around the circle **(Figure 2)**. Tighten the slipknot and slide out the cardboard.

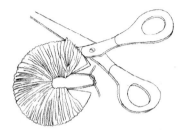

Figure 2

Trim your pom-pom: Create two more cardboard templates the same diameter as what you want your pom-pom to be. Sandwich your pom-pom between them and pierce the center with a tapestry needle to secure. Trim around the edges of the template **(Figure 3)**. Remove templates and needle to reveal your pom-pom!

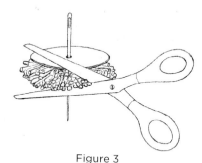

Figure 3

About the Yarns

Iceland

Icelandic Wool: Ístex

Used in Fridmar Hat (Plötulopi) and Ida Mitts (Lodband Einband)

The outstanding quality of Icelandic wool is legendary because it is superbly light and insulating. The Lodband Einband Lace and the Plötulopi in particular are no exception. The Lodband Einband is available in a range of stunning colors reminiscent of the dramatic Icelandic landscape itself: restless seas, volcanic beaches, lava flows, sunsets, hot springs, and pools. This is a strong, slightly unyielding yarn, but it is easy to work with, and there is certainly no snagging or splitting of the yarn.

Ideally suited to using in gradating bands of color, the Lodband Einband is perhaps not one that initially lends itself easily to two-color pattern work. However, once you familiarize yourself with it, you will be richly rewarded with a fabric that washes beautifully to reveal a scrunchy, springy, beautiful piece of knitting that will soften greatly with use and will be worn for warmth and endurance.

Knitting with the Plötulopi is quite an experience in itself. Unlike any other yarn, it arrives in the form of an aesthetically appealing "cake" that requires no preparation or winding into balls. Once you start knitting, it is as if you are working with a length of cloud: it is gossamer-light, ethereal, and unimaginably fragile. Approach the knitting with tenderness and you will succeed in a seamless piece of knitting with no breaks, joins, or knots. If you have never knitted with this yarn before, I strongly recommend a practice swatch before embarking on a whole project—you must hold the yarn carefully and knit each stitch with care—but I guarantee that you will develop a rhythm, and the knitting will grow quickly. Very careful washing will reveal its true cloudlike qualities as it develops bounce,

shimmer, and luster, and an unexpected but much appreciated strength. Your gossamer fine cloud of yarn is transformed into a soft, insulating, and durable fabric that gently whispers to you, "Wear me outdoors when it is cold and snowy."

Estonia

Kauni

Used in Anneli Doll and Liisi Cardigan

Based in Denmark with wool sourced from Estonia, Kauni makes 100% wool 8/2 yarn that is buttery soft and delectable in a jewel-like array of colors—there are more than seventy. It glides from the ball onto the needles and knits like a dream; its extraordinary yardage (350 m [383 yd]) ensures you will be able to carry on knitting and knitting and knitting. The fabric is rewardingly light, soft, and supple, and it plumps up nicely when carefully washed. With a good stitch definition, it is ideal for both one-color lace designs and stranded work—definitely a delight to work with.

Finland

Riihivilla

Used in Onni Hat, Onni Sweater, Tovio Hat, and Tovio Mittens

Riihivilla is a small family business in Finland that produces magical yarns using wool from their Finn Sheep flocks. Available in otherworldly, delicate shades that come in undyed shades as well as those dyed by using plants and mushrooms, this quietly simple yarn speaks to us of Finland's mossy forests, remote lakes, and wildly beautiful landscapes. The Finns have a true affinity with nature, and this is captured within Riihivillas yarn: it is rustic, soft, and yielding with a reassuring whiff of sheep that winds easily into balls and knits up beautifully. It creates fabric that has a traditionally old-fashioned look and feel and handles with a certain simplicity and charm. It is a yarn that has been produced with care from sheep to hank, and it will make the most precious and cosseting of projects for both adults and children. I have completely fallen under its spell and imagine you will, too.

Faroe Islands

Sirri 2-fold yarn

Used in Noomi Slippers, Oluffa Doorstop, and Marna Cape

Sirri's incredible Faroese two-fold Natural yarn is wildly robust and superbly hard wearing. With more than a whiff of the sheep remaining and bits and pieces of plant matter evident as you knit (all of which are easily picked out), this yarn importantly still has plenty of natural oils left on it. Consequently, it is easy to knit with and responds wonderfully to washing when its softer and more fragrant character is revealed. It is ideal for outdoor garments or projects that demand more wear and tear, such as slippers or house socks. It is available not only in soft natural tones but also cheerful, bright solid colors.

Sweden

Ullcentrum 2-thread yarn

Used in Freja Twined Scarf and Åsa Mittens

Ullcentrum is a small yarn manufacturer based on Öland, an island just off of Sweden's east coast, producing original, pure wool yarns from carefully selected Swedish wool sourced predominately from Öland or southern Sweden. Swedish wool is renowned for its strength and quality, and Ullcentrum spins only the softest and cleanest fleece to make their special yarns. Their 2-thread pure wool yarn, which is available in natural, variegated, and solid shades, has a soft, lustrous ap-

peal mixed with rugged, hard-working characteristics. This makes it an ideal yarn to work with for normal knitting, lace knitting, and twined knitting. It is strong enough to withstand the rigors of twisting and untwisting of twined knitting and its soft, sensuous side is revealed once washed. It is definitely enhanced after being firmly washed in really quite warm, verging on hot, soapy water (there is a slight amount of dye loss on the first wash, but it is minimal and does not affect other colors). Washing rewards you with a characterful, soft, firm, and elastic fabric if twined, and a springy and very wearable lace or stockinette stitch fabric. I strongly recommend that you try this yarn at least once—it is unique, and I have never met anyone who does not like it.

Shetland Islands

Shetland Wool: Jamieson & Smith

Used in Mootie Socks (2-ply jumper weight) and Dimitie Scarf (2-ply laceweight)

As you can image, any yarn shorn from the sheep that roam the Shetland Islands throughout the year, withstanding the wilds of a northerly winter far out at sea, will have considerable character and charm. Jamieson & Smith's two-ply jumper weight yarn is a sturdy, robust, and magnificently enduring yarn available in a cacophony of shades reminiscent of the constantly changing island light and of the encircling seas, cliffs, and heather.

Some might argue that pure Shetland wool is not for the fainthearted. This may well be true, as it is no way cashmere-soft; but it has rich rewards for the knitter who uses it. It is superbly easy to knit with, as there is definitely no splitting or snagging of the yarns. It is naturally perfect for Fair Isle and stranded knitting because the fibers draw the stitches together making a nice, slightly dense fabric. After washing, its true beauty will emerge: both the yarn and the colors will soften, noticeably releasing its own sweet "halo." You will go on wearing your Shetland knits for many winters to come because Shetland yarn is designed to last!

The two-ply lace yarn is a finer, slightly more restrained relative of the jumper-weight yarn, available in fewer colors. I favor the natural hues, which have their own unique beauty.

Norway

Hifa Trollgarn

Used in Oda Baby Blanket

The Norwegian family-owned company Hillesvåg Ullvarefabrikk AS has been making high-quality woolen yarns for more than a hundred years. Their appropriately named Trollgarn (Troll Yarn!) is a superb, large, lofty, soft, and springy two-ply yarn. Available in sumptuous colors, it is a high-quality yarn that behaves impeccably when knitted—so well in fact, that I did not need to wash the blanket after it was finished; I gave it only the lightest of presses. Trollgarn is easy to knit with, and it is warm and comforting.

Dale of Norway Heilo

Used in Nanna Twined Mitts

Dale of Norway has been producing high-quality woolen yarn from its factories in Dale (just outside of Bergen) since 1879; and their classic, pure Norwegian wool Heilo yarn has been in production since 1938. It is a classic, elegant, well-behaved yarn that is eminently easy to knit with and perfectly suited to classic, understated projects. Available in an inspiring range of colors including Norwegian blues, grays, and reds, the yarn is easy to use directly from the ball and behaves impeccably when twined, creating firm, lustrous, pronounced stitches. Washing will help to settle the fabric but does not change its characteristics noticeably. It has a soft, high-quality density that is reminiscent of classic vintage knitwear.

Denmark

Isager

Used in Adda Socks and Rya Flower Cushion

Marianne Isager is one of Denmark's most prolific knitwear designers whose pure woolen yarns are sophisticated, elegant, strong, and resilient. Available in a superb range of colors evocative of the unique landscapes of northern Denmark, where Marianne has her home and one of her shops, the fine-weight Tvinni and Spinni yarns are eminently suitable for fine-gauge knits. Used double, as I have done, they create a thicker, more substantial gauge. Easy to wind from the hank and with absolutely no splitting or snagging, the yarns knit up easily and respond well to careful washing and blocking. These yarns truly encapsulate a little bit of Denmark and the aesthetic of function and beauty.

Resources

IN THE UNITED STATES

Dale of Norway
4750 Shelburne Rd.
Ste. 20
Shelburne, VT 05482
www.dalegarn.no

Isager
10 Domingo Rd.
Santa Fe, NM 87508
www.knitisager.com

Nordic Fiber Arts
4 Cutts Rd.
Durham, NH 03824
(603) 868-1196
www.nordicfiberarts.com

Schoolhouse Press
(800) 968-5648
www.schoolhousepress.com

OUTSIDE THE UNITED STATES

Faroe Knitting
Bringsnagoeta 5, ovast
FO-100 Tórshavn
Faroe Islands
www.faroeknitting.com

Hillesvåg Ullvarefabrikk AS
Leknesvegen 259
NO-5915 Hjelmås
Norway
www.ull.no

Ístex
PO Box 140
270 Mosfellsbær
Iceland
www.istex.is

Jamieson & Smith
90 North Rd.
Lerwick, Shetland Isles
ZE1 OPQ
www.shetlandwool.org

Kauni
Odderbækvej 13
Fuglsang
7323 Give
Denmark
www.kauni.com

Riihivilla
Koskentie 774
25560 Koski as
Finland
www.riihivilla.com

Sirri
Áarvegur 12
Postboks 271
FO-100 Tórshavn
Faroe Islands
www.sirri.fo

Ullcentrum Öland
Byrumvagen 59
SE-38074 Löttorp
Sweden
www.ullcentrum.com

Index

Knit one, take two
WITH THESE OTHER KNITTABLE TITLES FROM INTERWEAVE

NORTHERN KNITS
Designs Inspired by the
Knitting Traditions of
Scandinavia, Iceland, and
the Shetland Isles

Lucinda Guy

ISBN 978-1-59668-171-2
$24.95

NEW ENGLAND KNITS
Timeless Knitwear with
a Modern Twist

Cecily Glowik MacDonald and
Melissa LaBarre

ISBN 978-1-59668-180-4
$24.95

VINTAGE MODERN KNITS
Contemporary Designs Using
Classic Techniques

Courtney Kelley and Kate
Gagnon Osborn

ISBN 978-1-59668-240-5
$24.95

shop.knittingdaily.com

From cover to cover, *Interweave Knits* magazine
presents great projects for the beginner to the
advanced knitter. Every issue is packed full of
captivating smart designs, step-by-step instructions,
easy-to-understand illustrations, plus well-written,
lively articles sure to inspire. **Interweaveknits.com**

Join Knittingdaily.com, an online community
that shares your passion for knitting. You'll get
a free e-newsletter, free patterns, projects store,
a daily blog, event updates, galleries, tips and
techniques, and more. Sign up for *Knitting Daily*
at **knittingdaily.com**.

Northern Knits Gifts

Thoughtful Projects

INSPIRED BY FOLK TRADITIONS

LUCINDA GUY

EDITOR ERICA SMITH

TECHNICAL EDITOR AND ILLUSTRATOR
THERESE CHYNOWETH

ART DIRECTOR LIZ QUAN

COVER & INTERIOR DESIGN LORA LAMM

PRODUCTION KATHERINE JACKSON

PHOTOGRAPHER JOE HANCOCK

Interweave Press LLC
201 East Fourth Street
Loveland, CO 80537
Interweave.com

Printed in China by C & C Offset

Library of Congress Cataloging-in-Publication Data

Guy, Lucinda.
  Northern knits gifts : thoughtful projects inspired by folk
traditions / Lucinda Guy.
     pages cm
  ISBN 978-1-59668-562-8 (pbk.)
  1. Knitting--Patterns. 2. Knitting--Europe, Northern. 3.
Knitwear--Design--Themes, motives. 4. Wool fabrics. I. Title.
  TT819.E853G89 2012
  746.43'2--dc23

                    2012017923

10 9 8 7 6 5 4 3 2 1

For François

I am deeply grateful to everyone at Interweave for
making this book possible.

I extend heartfelt thanks to everyone involved, and
especially François, for all their help, expertise,
patience, and support.

I also owe a considerable debt of gratitude to all the
yarn companies who so generously supplied me with
wonderful woolen yarns.